UNITED POEMS OF AMERICA

Poetry for United States' Semiquincentennial/
America's 250th Birthday

by

JOHN DAVID THOMPSON

All poems written by John David Thompson
UNITED POEMS OF AMERICA
Poetry project conceived by John David Thompson

Cover design and graphics by Karisa Runkel

Manufactured in the United States of America.
Digitally published and available on Amazon.com
through Kindle Direct Publishing
via BLUE JAY'S BUNGALOW PRESS, Bloomfield, IA

ISBN (13-digit): 978-1-73286-656-0
ISBN (10-digit): 1-73286-656-2

Library of Congress Control Number: 2025912227

Email author: upoemsofamerica@yahoo.com

John David Thompson is the author of 18 books, 17 of which are poetry.
He holds an MFA in Creative Writing/Poetry from New England College
The poet/educator lives in Bloomfield, Iowa.

Some of the poems in *United Poems of America* have appeared
in previous collections of the poet.

Note/Disclaimer: Trademark words and phrases are for creative writing/
poetry purposes only.
Any omitted trademark signs are unintended.

United Poems of America first manufactured on
KINDLE DIRECT PUBLISHING

TABLE OF CONTENTS

*Acknowledgments

Poems in this book are previously unpublished except the following:

1832-Portrait of Chief Black Hawk (99 Voices, 99 Lives: County Poems of Iowa)

1838-Black-Eyed Susan (Hidden Voices from Hush-a-bye Rooms)

1903-Kitty Hawk (A Reed Grows in Carolina)

1912-A Partial Colossus (Titanic: A Centenarian Voyage in Verse)

1932-Hooverville (99 Voices, 99 Lives: County Poems of Iowa)

1936-Rose of Sharon (Winter Maria)

1944-Anne Frank of the Attic (Winter Maria)

1956-The Pelvis of Elvis (Whatever Happened to Baby Boom?)

1963-For Whom the Grass Knolls (Whatever Happened to Baby Boom?)

1971-One Indian, Crying (Whatever Happened to Baby Boom?)

1974-I've Written a Letter to Nixon (Whatever Happened to Baby Boom?)

1984-On the Subway with Bernhard Goetz (Tender Revolutions)

1986-Christa McAuliffe at Liftoff (Whatever Happened to Baby Boom?)

1997-Monica Lewinsky's Dress (Whatever Happened to Baby Boom?)

2001-The Eleventh of September (Love Letter from Luxembourg)

2012-School Shooting 101, formerly titled Because It Can't Stop Now, (Whatever Happened to Baby Boom?)

2021-Cancel Culture Catches Up to the Statue of Liberty (Whatever Happened to Baby Boom?)

By the rude bridge that arched the flood,
Their flag to April's breeze unfurled,
Here once the embattled farmers stood
And fired the shot heard round the world.

— Ralph Waldo Emerson
from *Concord Hymn*
Battles of Lexington and Concord, 1775

This book of poetry is dedicated to

Laura & Lyle

Chris & Keegan

Lindsay & Melody

Kathie & John

Marian & Maureen

(And my fellow Americans)

UNITED POEMS OF AMERICA

ABOUT THE AUTHOR

John David Thompson is the author of 18 books, 17 of which are poetry, including

TITANIC: A CENTENARIAN VOYAGE IN VERSE

WINTER MARIA

WHATEVER HAPPENED TO BABY BOOM?

Thompson's poetry has appeared in T*he Iowan, The Des Moines Register, Harvard Review* and other publications throughout the state and nation. Born and raised in southern Iowa, he enjoys traveling and researching the state and nation in search of ideas and inspiration for poems. He holds an MFA in Creative Writing/Poetry from New England College and has completed post-graduate coursework in Poetry at the Harvard Creative Writing Program and the University of Iowa Writers' Workshop, both with honors. Many of his books of poetry have been collected and archived at the State Library of Iowa, the State Historical Library of Iowa, and other literary institutions throughout the state of Iowa. Thompson currently lives and teaches in central Iowa at the secondary level.

The poet may be reached at
upoemsofamerica@yahoo.com

Thompson's books can be found and purchased on his author website:
johndavidthompson.com

1776

Do You Have Something to Declare?

Quill pen over sword,

Mind over musket—

in theory,
we kill the king

by abolition of each colony,

establishment of state.

In this honorable hall, first house of customs—
we have gathered our brethren bags

to declare: independence.

What sufferance
we have patiently harbored—

darkens, seeps, and leaves

                    toward its original Sea of Tyranny.

The chariot of summer arcs its inalienable light of high horses.
Hooves of divine Providence
thrust voice upon each clapping cloud—

a new nation, a new day.

1777

Battle of Saratoga

I-FREEMAN'S FARM

Seeking to divide-and-conquer the Hudson River Valley,
sequester New England from southern colonies,
the British learned a Greek lesson
from the redoubtable patriots,
downwind, small village of Saratoga
on Freeman's Farm.

It was a Pyrrhic victory, at best.

The felling trees, torched bridges,
bloodied redcoats tattered on late summer ground—

'Gentlemen Johnny' and his champagne retinue
blindly flew into the concealed woods with bayonets,
yet the direct hits on American wildlife there— were few.

True. The Brit militia may have held that abandoned farm,
but their casualties planted a fertile field
for colonial reinforcements to harvest, come autumn.

II-BEMIS HEIGHTS

The first surrender, like first cut, is deepest.
Its white-flagged tongue flaps as a wounded bird
above encampments, countryside, and one ocean. Europe is all ears.

A harvest moon, a hunter's moon—
short on supply and refurbished men, British artillery pieces make a move.

Premier of the frontier rifle awaits them at Bemis Heights.

In the aftermath, General Horatio Gates, even Benedict Arnold rival
Continental Army Commander-in-Chief George Washington
in colonial popularity after the upstate win.

Perhaps of most import, the turn-point triumph impresses the French.

1778

Valley Forge

Nothing here forges.

The iron will of winter
hammers, beats, and shapes
the cold landscape, since December last.

Most of my men are shoeless.
On the sloping ground, bloodied naked tracks
invite the merest rodent
to a curious rouse.

Even my chestnut charger, Nelson, is better hooved
for the Harshness in Arms.

True. Our pokes at the redcoats have been necessary—
but not sufficient to exterminate the war.

The British remain pesky and significant from harbor to field.
Congress has fled an occupied Philadelphia like a fury of wives.

Influenza, typhoid, and dysentery dogs the encampment.
like a three-headed beast from Underneath.

Yet, there is leverage, advantage here
if we do not waste in the abundance of thin provisions.

The valley is high, a defensible plateau.
Should the Brits encroach through impassable roads of snow,
we will see their colors coming.

And logs of winter, they lumber long.
My troops have time, time to train—
perfect the bayonet, form a more kill-efficient line.

In spring, we will doff the parasitic frost,
descend a thawed, ready-jawed army
for triumphant climb.

1779

Legless Benedict

The difficulty of it all
is the ease of treason,
breaded trail of betrayal,
aggregate rationale
that builds and builds
until one must stamp and act
on one's own.

An enterprising, regaled general,
am I not America's King Richard III—
literally giving life-limb
in distraught need
of a supportive horse?

The cracked egg of an unstable nation
is yolk empty.

My sense as a sea trader—
intrepid conquests in Canada—
my successful second leg at Saratoga—
have all but secured the sacred Hudson River Valley
for the States' campaigns.

And, yet, I am overlooked like unpraised rain.
Junior officers receive promotion at the speed of musket-shot.

My merits are lost in herd trot of a winter reprieve.

Blessed with tit-for-tat's disease,
I possess a smuggle up my House-of-Handover sleeve.

My latest orders read Washington wants to orphan me out
to command a fledgling West Point.

I shall not stand for it.
I'll give it to the British on a plate garnished with switchgrass.
I'll sell out, surrender the joint.

1780

New England's Dark Day

Common sense claims it is broad day.
Noon is nocturnal. The weather revolts.
All field flowers close.
Even the Dutchman has folded its breeches.

Sin in its midday darkness. Guilt bearing a cape of opaque gray.

The cordwainer abandons his finest leather, orphans a new shoe.

We colonists head for frothy taverns, meeting houses, and churches
to pray for light's redemption.

Forgive us, Lord. Forgive us, King.
We fled Our Mother. We departed on perilous, proud ships.
Now, is bleak hour of Judgment.

Or are these flakes of coal on our quivering lips?

Is this Notus' handiwork, the god of south wind, blowing—
burned leaves from British siege of Carolina's Charleston?

Have we been Friday's fools for such reactionary,
transcendental reliance?

It appears that when First Crew loaded the Mayflower cabin trunks,

someone forgot to pack the science.

1781

Siege of Yorktown

A snowy egret surrenders
its white plume to a fleet of clouds
occluding the quiet mouth
of Chesapeake Bay.

The persistent teeth of Washington
converge a conquest of colonial soldiers
from bloodied North's tried and tested fields.

Even the visiting French are relentless
in getting a grip, bottling up the Brits.

Cornwallis calls in sick.

A second-hand officer lays down the king's sword.

In a town-hall steeple, upstream, a chime—thirteen times.

The Articles of Confederation constitute the nation.

It is time to end the war.

1782

Great Seal of the United States

Evidently, it is the bald eagle,
our national bird, that bears
the hefty lifting, here.
Its talons teem in clutches of thirteen—
liberty's defensive, upward arrows
and preferred olive leaves of peace.
Devised, designed, displayed
in a new-world order of red-and-white striped heraldry,
the shield—coat of arms—blazons a chief of starless blue.
Backed by an unfinished pyramid, Eye of Providence,
indeed, there is climbing to do.
All hail, the Republic's raptor, its service-breast beneath Glory's sun.
And in its beak, scrolls a unified speech: Out of Many, One.

1783

The Treaty of Paris in Partial Oils

American Commissioners of the Preliminary Peace Negotiations with Great Britain, painting in absolutus by Benjamin West

What is a work
if its product is left unfinished—
a hope in abeyant happening,
a brush with abandonment,
a silver gorget plate of sour grapes?

A profile of Americans sits in Paris—
with their manifest papers, independent pens—
Adams, a fix of Franklins, Jay, and Laurens.

Alas, the British aren't coming,
which translates, their gutted diplomats aren't posing—
and what with primed casts
of frontier Founding Fathers
dried and done upon canvas' landscape.

The lower-right fragment of the unexecuted frame
stirs like a nebulous banshee from the Atlantic,
adumbrates in cloud-shape of the Great Mother Isle
herself in gray's doting age.

1784

Benjamin Franklin's Face-Value Invention

It's *nearly* impossible to check if Ben invented these specs,

but Poor Richard's eyes sure made them a *far-sight* popular.

1785

The Dollar Is Currency

The corpulent colonists
with weighty issues
should be tenfold pleased:

it replaces the pound.

1786

Shays' Rebellion

Chaos is the first child
of a birthing nation.

It cries for juice and justice.
It disconnects harmony and hook
from precious cradle.

Colonial soldiers lay down their arms—
pick up scythe, sickle, flail and hand-plow.

But the fledgling government
is not seeded in green, rooted in coin.
Debt grows in Pelham farm dirt.
A supplier in Boston wants paid.

The Articles of Confederation quivers with holes
on thin, untenable paper.

Enter Chaos, quietly, crawling
if it so please debtors' court,
with a fleet of grievances,
a stalk of documents.

Suggestion of reform leads to claims of radicalism.

Contingents of countrymen seize courthouses,
block judges from assuming robed thrones
for a mighty wage.

A farmer named Daniel Shays emerges
as top prong of insurgent pitchfork.
An arsenal is attacked. Hills teem with rebels.

The tax-fat statehouse must tighten its bully-belt.
A prime moulding of the *Constitution* is framed.

1787

If the First Farmers Had Framed the Preamble to the *Constitution*

Us the folks—
‘cuz we want a darn good country
hear-call for a justice o’ peace and some big guns
in the forest and a few more in town
that any fella could use if he had to,
to make us all get along
so God don’t get mad at us and
make our women barren—
yep, we tickle
the feathers of this fancy pen
on this here skinny letter
in this smelly hall
we done borrowed all summerz long from
the fine folks of Pensylvania.

1788

King George III Descends into Lunacy

What will ships heading for America,
the new country,
with their textiles and trims—
yes, what will the frigates say
of the old king's madness?

Will it even be of import
among luxury exports
of trade and exchanges?

It is late 1788.
The *Constitution* ratified.

Abroad, among the British,
the nettlesome news is confirmed.

King George III is terrified.

A mania overwhelms him.

He rules in his bedclothes
crowned with a hectic pillowcase.

Barmy and bonkers,
the monarch flits in fits
between the sweaty, surrendering sheets.

Why, the entire House of Hanover is a spiral staircase.

And, this gives those with eyes on his throne, *the creeps.*

1789

The Merry and the Miserable

These are hours of solemnity, celebration
in new America.
Our hopes, desires, prayers
transcend to a jubilant checklist
of things done:

- Inaugurate Washington as first president. √
- Create a system of departments-State, Treasury, and War. √
- Call to order a service of courts. √
- Lay the foundation for the Bill of Rights. √

Yes, in the victorious States,
dutiful citizens are wheeling an oath of red, white, and blue threads.
But, abroad, in France,
a needful stomach fingers a loaf of bread.
The bones of the proletariat pitted against the King's ordained throne.
A revolution assembles.
Hunger and horror in the streets commence to wheel.
It looks like rain in Paris—this coming decade.
Thundering clouds of liberty, equality, fraternity
storm the castle of Bastille.

1790

The Death of Benjamin Franklin

Among his inventions,
Benjamin Franklin did not conceive death.

It has preceded him. It will succeed him.

The First American's soul
joins the white foam—of its inevitable wake.

It was pleurisy, wasn't it?

A bursting of the lungs that brought
the indefatigable patriot down.

Fitting perhaps—the apprentice printer,
Franklin was incessantly bursting
with new ideas to frame for the fresh nation.

Born in Boston,
buried in Philadelphia,
his luminous legacy forged a kind of colonial highway
until, at last, democracy had settled, home.

Literary, electric, pensive, fireproof, *armonic*—
Franklin was a statesman...every cobblestone step of the pave.

A dying man can do nothing easily—
Poor Richard's last words.

The gray mourners form a shadow parade.
Part of the town buries itself.

A child's kite flies over his grave.

1791

Then, Imagine a Bill of Wrongs

You can't go to church there, and don't complain about it in press or assembly.

Guns are unbearable. Make a lit stockpile of the bangers in the town square.

The soldiers are sleeping over, whenever. Lock up your whiskey and wives.

Your home is Congress' castle, and they're getting frisky with it.

You're innocent in Spring, guilty in Fall. We don't need no stinking evidence.

You've been accused of something by somebody. A lawyer's here somewhere.

Heads, you get a judgmental jury. Tails, an injurious judge.

You want to see the light of day? That'll be $500 million, and a whooping.

You see this right, and the 9 rights above and below? They're your only rights.

If the government forgot to put in enough power now, we'll put more in later.

1792

Cornerstone, United States Executive Mansion

If you read the *Bible* and apply more literally,

I am the sandstone rock of the new federal city,

fresh seat of democracy, and the burgeoning free world.

Upon me,

the weight of fine mason's frame and a young nation.

This Irish-born architect Hoban, I trust him.

He bears a sculptor's hands.

With each block, arch and Ionic column,

I feel as if I am holding magnificence,

uniting all walls known

to post-colonial humankind.

President Washington himself,

in blue and buff wool coat, musketeer boots,

presiding over L'Enfant's select landscape

navigating the grounds like crossing the Delaware,

overseeing each turn of raw material, steering about.

Ironic bend on Potomac River—He will never reside here.

Washington will never live in Washington. Georgeless town.

The not-yet-nicknamed White House, a heralded home to all other presidents.

1793

Fugitive Slave Act of 1793

It is not so much Congress—
as a it is a clause—
yes, a clause in the *U. S. Constitution,*
a passage to regression
and chains.

Any runaway slave
harbored in a free or hideaway state
is to be delivered and claimed
back to slack whippings
of Plantation's pain.

The public rails for amendment
to such a skin-splitting thorn
and waits for an Underground spring
where Harriet Tubman is born.

1794

Whiskey Rebellion

If the new nation is a wide-eyed pupil,
this is its first test.

Imposed upon
the frontier farmer,
breaking soil and raising grains
for the citizens of a young country—

a tax, a tax—and domestic at that!

This is a fighting word, a fiery claim.

What is the indigent plow to do—
furrow into the silver clouds of heaven
to make it coin-rain?

True.
Federal government is mired in war debt.

And yet,
where is good spirit in levying home-grown spirits?

What is so civil about charging each liquor still?

In western Pennsylvania,
an insurgence of lit pitchforks
insurrects on a hill—
This excise tax from Congress be damned to the dram!

Enter from mounted eastern front,
Washington and Hamilton's mighty Federalist militia.

In a matter of minuteman minutes, the revolt disperses.
The Stars-and-Stripes student passes its initial exam.

1795

Pick a Treaty, Any Treaty

Jay Treaty

I remember my junior-high social studies teacher trying to explain this. And I thought to myself, *Why are we even talking to the British? And what is a Chief Justice of the Supreme Court doing by going over there and settling anything?* But American ships were sinking in the Great Atlantic, and the Brits were still itching like dandruff in our new-nation hair in the Northwest Territory. Evidently, America could give Mother England a cold winter,
but not a cold shoulder.

Pinckney's Treaty

Let's face it. With this treaty, the United States landed a free foot in the port of then-Spanish New Orleans, while the eagle's' beak was salivating to get its claws on West and East Florida.

Greenville Treaty

If this were on *Jeopardy™*, *What is the Greenville Treaty?* would, no doubt, be a $2,000 question to this answer.
Native Americans were thrown a fallen timber, sleeping bone along the shores of the Great Lakes in exchange for ceding what would become sizable portions of Michigan, Illinois, Indiana, and most of Ohio.

1796

Get the Political Parties Started

In general (as general),

Washington warned against this and these—

the ineludible rise and slime

of the Janus-faced, two-headed political party system

flinging its beastly ballots across the congressional floor,

the American countryside.

This forefather foretold it:

Federalists, Democratic-Republicans picking candidates

out of his Cabinet like fine ceramic stoneware;

Adams and Jefferson duking it out like patriotic pugilists

over a centralized government, states' rights—

whether to embrace or ignore the taxing Mother Country;

a double-masked donning of chaotic order

with more split platforms, debates, and parties to come.

It makes contradictory sense, after all.

Isn't the phrase *United States,*

our world's biggest oxymoron?

1797

Begin the Navy

Troubled water—
it was not just for a bridge
over which a Simon & Garfunkel ballad
to pass under.

No.
Troubled water had hampered and seized
young American merchant ships
venturing to make a trade-name for themselves
in the turbulent churl of great Atlantic.

Like the sky needs a sheet of blue,
a nation needs a fleet of Navy.

It takes the launching of congressional act— and first ship.
That's it.

A frigate actually—
full of sail, firepower, and voyage boys—
the first aptly named *USS United States*.

USSs Constellation and *Constitution* soon followed,
waterlines launched from hearth's harbor—
out onto the perilous seas
where British royal deckers, French vessels, and corsairs
waited and waded for salty-gun battle.

Heave-a-ho, there sailor,
in due time,
anchors be aweighed, admirals be commissioned,
torpedoes be damned.

Upon waters, you wrestle
for peace upon your homeland.

1798

Alien and Sedition Acts

La guerre couvait en mer avec les Francais.
War was brewing at sea with the French.
Donc, si les citoyens amèricans voulaient
toujours parler anglaise,
So, if Americans still wanted to speak English,
il incombait au Congrès d'adopter les lois
sur Les Etrangers et Les Seditions.
it behooved Congress to pass
the Alien and Sedition Acts.
Cette immigration bloquée
This bottlenecked immigration,
discours rebelle bâilloné contre les fédéralistes,
gagged rebellious speech against the Federalists,
et a permis à des millions d'enfants americains
de réusssir beaucoup plus facilment les cours
de langue requis
and made it much easier for millions
of American children to pass requisite language courses
sans sous-tiles.
without subtitles.

1799

Passing the War Debt to American Farmers

There is no such thing as a free musket.

"Brown Bess" herself cost a couple of quid
to fire through her smoothbore passage.

The long rifle and bayonet commanded Continental costs as well—
not to mention the Spanish dollars and endless pence
needed to feed and fit the troops.

The new naval frigates gunning French masts
during the Quasi-War in the West Indies—
their victorious decks did not float on forgivable loans.

Indebtedness, again, turned its collective shadow
toward the American farmer, landowner
in the form of an empty-hat tax.
The values of the Pennsylvania Dutch homes were assessed
based on the number of windows.
Thus, the Window Tax is born.

Imagine, assessors on horseback—many of them Quakers, Moravians—
counting framed glass while dodging furious stones.

1800

Library of Congress

Among the amazing "fyi" facts
shelved at the Library of Congress,
since its turn-of-the-century inception,
is its possession of the world's smallest book,
a 1985 edition of "Old King Cole,"
a nursery rhyme
with book print, 1 mm X 1 mm,
give or take a speck,
roughly the size of a pencil point,
or period—
and, below
posits a copy of it

.

trust me, it's in there

1801

District of Columbia Organic Act

Well, of course, a country needs a capital—
a place of location, power, marbled columns, gilded domes,
somewhere to carve dead presidents,
erect subliminal monuments to penetrate
the no-fly-by sky.
And a judicious river should execute through it
like a school of red herring
spawning the Congressional-controlled cause.
Here, both houses will legislatively rest
to 24/7 worldwide scrutiny,
and adjourning applause.

1802

First Week at West Point

You arrive in July,
take a solemn oath
that begins with *I*,
swear to defend and protect
the *Constitution* against
foreign and domestic effects,
receive PT uniforms, get your hair cut out of joint,
do whatever's issued to you,
compete for company points,
train for six weeks beneath a basic sun—
deadlift, power throw, push-up,
sprint-drag-carry, plank, and two-mile run,
consider career pathways, do military math,
bond with other cadets, speak with sage seniors,
so you can best leaf on a service branch,
take on menial tasks with soldiers calling you *plebe*,
scrub floors, call the minutes, sort laundry, set that table—
then collapse in camouflage on a cot.

That's why they call them *fatigues.*

1803

Louisiana Purchase

In short,
Napoleon was cash-strapped
like sans-culottes
in a red liberty cap.

Enslaved plantation workers revolted
in Saint Domingue,
leaving coffee, sugar, cotton, and indigo
in fields and trees—unharvested.

Unfinanced from Caribbean mishap,
Le Petit Corporal pondered
France's impending poverty
in Parisian palace, rose water bath.

He put *deux* and *deux* together
among sudsy expand.
La Grande Armėe would need money to battle Britain.
The Americans wanted westward land.

Four cents per acre—
the diminutive cost command.
Throw in Port of New Orleans,
and, in displacement distance, Custer's Last Stand.

President Jefferson took the threat
of British gripping invasion
in North America, from Canada,
off the French cravat, or France's neckband.

With the Mississippi River a flowing freebie,
the Bread Basket of the World was born
with amber waves of God's golden strands.
(By the way, *condamner* is the French word for *damn*.)

1804

Burr-Hamilton Duel

It was a pinnacle of things,
a culmination of animosities,
personal and political,
that triggered agreement to duel,
an unlock of flintlocks,
demand for satisfaction.

Burr had been just that: a bur.
His encroaching ambitions,
burrowing beneath my skin and skull—
blaming me, Federalist rivals
for his drawbacks and gremlins.

Our serpent history uncoiled
from elections to appointments,
public insults to private impasse.

But I did not want this fire,
this noose-walk of ten paces.

At first light,
with my letters and prayers in order,
I rowed on the Hudson River to Weehawken,
shook hands with a despicable outlaw,
and sought the Divine.

I turned and shot a-loft, in an innocuous tree.
The Vice President's bullet entered my abdomen.
(How many American citizens can ever phrase that?)

I died the next day, gasping for honor—nothing further—
with Thomas Jefferson's right-hand man
wanted for murder.

1805

Sacagawea

Kidnapped from the high grasses
of my Shoshone people,
I am asked, not to return,
but to pilot through,
these military explorers
in their Corps of Discovery,
past my homeland, a Continental Divide—
forging a great waterway, patriots' passage
to a relentless sea.

In a keelboat and pair of pirogues,
we course our way to stay-put Rockies,
where tongue-trade exchanges oars
for a negotiation of horses.

I speak in rivers,
translate in peace.

An infant child at my bosom
calms the mistrust of stolen mountains.

Our quiet, hush-a-bye skins,
a guide of smothering white.

Mark of unchartered flora and fauna—
blue flax and bighorn sheep—
I point where a rigor of waves clap
upon untrammeled cliffs
quaking a symphony of foam-rends.

Unlike limits of my captivity,
the unlimited territory ends.

1806

Lewis and Clark Expedition

Among the encumbrances, obstructions, impediments
bracing Lewis and Clark
on their excruciating excursion
to Northwest Passage,
aphasia, or a speech impediment,
was not one of them.

The captain and second lieutenant
sought a specific ocean,
the Pacific Ocean—
the specific Pacific Ocean.

1807

Impressment

Like a French whore
in a foreign port,
the Admiral Lord
of British Royal Navy
was looking
to put the foul squeeze on
a few qualified seamen.

1808

Birth of American Industrial Revolution

It only took a spark,
a whit of coal
to get America's industrial era burning.

A judge in Pennsylvania, Jesse Fell,
experimented with the carbon carrier
by placing a bit of it
inside an iron grate
one February night.

Then, he fell asleep—
waking to a glorious, storied
containment of fire.

And what of wood?

Its room-consuming, rotting pile
was shown the backyard
where it was given a second-wind hire:

the campfire.

1809

American Weaver

To the milliner's delight, a practical hat
Its straw brim, too, compared to summer's day
Designed by silk weave—a lovely, temperate cross-hatch
Entwined with honey-thread, a blade of field hay
Why, Athena would be pleased; Arachne's head spun
With its rise of golden flax crown, sensible brim
To shade noggin and face from piercing sun
As if patriot skulls given a manger of hay, Biblical inn

Hats off to Mary Dixon Kies, sunburn's combatant
For inventing a braid to shield blaze and storm
The first woman, US, to secure a federal patent .
Of wide use—capping the farm plow and school uniform
An idiom's tip-of-the-hat to conclude fair sonnet
Bless the coming of rays, donning of fine-fiber bonnet

1810

To Catch a Horse Thief, to Trap a Beaver

The post-colonial period of America was also an age
of seizure:

arms,
weapons,
homesteads,
native lands,
ports,
sailors,
even the animals—
domestic and riparian.

Horse thievery was so commonplace in commonwealths and states
that select societies were established to apprehend
stallion stealers.

Vigilant citizens volunteered to sit and watch
napping neighers.

If a midnight pony was taken,
the heaviest of townsfolk, allegedly, would venture after it
on the speediest mount possible.
Then, the fat captor would sit on lean thief
until a posse of justice arrived.

As for the beaver,
a worldwide demand for its fur, particularly on hats,
put law on the other side of rustling water.
A furrier like John Jacob Astor could bank on it.

Trapping the pelted paddlers was not only legal,
but fashionable and profitable.
Why, anytime the thickset, whiskered river engineer swam toward
an underwater, toothed-trigger, it was a voyage of the dammed.

1811

Slave Revolt, Whitney Plantation Memorial, Louisiana

Like Boston tea,
we steeped and seeped
into the free-foam sea.

With machete and musket
in broken-back hands,
we waded to trouble coast-water.

The plantation rains came
before we cleared to Orleans,
gun-hungry locals, the military pounding.

They must've killed
Charles a thousand times—
chopped off his hands, shot up his thighs.

You stay put, boy—
or, that's what you get
for walking.

We are riveted spirits, now—
each of our carved heads
rigged like a jester's marotte

on a pond-dwelling pole.

Here swims memory
within emancipated soul.

Hush, now. Slavery's long been beheaded.

No talking.

1812

The War of 1812

To study early America is to consider the British,
territorial-teated Mother Country,
empire by insatiable sea.

And there must be some discrete name, terminology
for surrendering one's young—*title waive*—perhaps, no?

Whatever it is—I don't think she, initially, meant it.

(Sing to Tchaikovsky)
The reasons for this war were manifold.
The reasons for this war were manifold.

Impressment,
ingratiation with natives,
interference with French trade,
imperialistic tendencies to rule Canada,
invoking a need to claim, defend national honor—
the five I's of incivilities.

England had become North America's dire wolf—
the republic's consensus being to remove its hideous claw
from the continental den, permanently.

All things being equal,
this was the Second War of Independence,
our country's first sequel.

Perhaps the American Revolution was classic,
but mere overture.

1813

Capture of USS *Chesapeake*

Proteus, the sea-change god,
he—alone—must be my overlord, protector.

Chased, captured, commandeered
in mere minutes at Boston Harbor
by a waiting British frigate,

I shift as the winds that anchored my demise.

My men down, my ensign in tatters,
I renounce my proud prefix, *USS*,
to *HMS* in service to Royal Navy—
in less than a maritime hour.

It is one matter to lose.

It is quite the other to be forced to play,
to carry cannon for the other side.

In the conscripted years ahead,
I sail, an unwilling traitor,

until I am, at last, dressed down in England,
torn into timber, fragments of forest,

shaped into a Wickham watermill
bearing my shame and namesake,
my longleaf pine providing
the foundation for flour, animal seed.

Yes, in time, I will be broken,
morphed into a kind of grinding misery,
a million masts away
from my glorious graze at sea.

1814

The Raising of the Muse

I did not expect to be awakened—
not this September morning—
after incessant cannon fire,
burst-bomb of shells,
a trajectory theater of rockets
beaming toward the fort
from a dark harbor.

No.
With recent incineration at the nation's capital,
the president's mansion charred and blazed—portraits in ruins,
I thought I had folded,
my creases of dyed wool,
white cotton—waiting to be burned.

Then, a spangle of sunlight arrives. Tomorrow has survived.
I feel the formality of garrison hands, American soldiers
stretching my stripes for a good yawn.

The smaller storm flag that endured
all battles of night, lowers,
as I am hoisted up bastion's flagpole
above the smoke-scarred ramparts.

O, I look out, and what do my starry eyes see?
A man with a spyglass, from a distant truce ship—
he is staring at me.

I wave to good patriot across Chesapeake Bay.

He lifts a paper and pen. By dawn's early light, he begins.

Indeed, this will be a banner day.

1815

Battle of New Orleans

News was a slow-moving vessel in 1815—
1814, for that matter,
when a delegation of British, American dignitaries
gathered in Ghent on Christmas Eve to cease the war.

Later that winter,
in uninformed, uniformed New Orleans,
out-of-loop, clueless coats from the United Kingdom
encroached upon Chalmette Plantation—
where a melting pot of Old Hickory militia—
smugglers, pirates, homegrown bayou-brave yeomen
hid behind cotton bales,
fired well-timed squirrel guns—
sending the swamp predators
up a winless river, engulfed in defeat.

Yes, news back in the day was a slothful ship.

How to tell all of Europe, the Crown is down.
Napoleon will earn his comeuppance, too.
Here, in this bottle, a message, one word, surging eastward, Atlantic—
Waterloo

1816

The Year Without a Summer

Like a single footprint,
a volcanic eruption is a geological event
that can change the course of wisdom, water
or weather.

In April, 1815,
Mount Tambora, the two-headed drum,
blew her sticks and stack
with global repercussions.

An umbrella of ash spread its pumice and sulfur
across the green, unsuspecting globe.

The after-effects of mutinous magma,
both imminent and subtlc, postponed.

On the Dutch East Indies archipelago,
a mass of magma chased natives
down to the fleeting bone.

A cold, summer-seized year later
in America,

President Thomas Jefferson himself—
with a failed wheat crop, in a scape of gray,
before, behind, beneath him—
stood hat-in-hand,
in line with an overflow or farmers, broke brothers
at an agrarian bank,
applying for a loan.

1817

Goodbye, Dolley

Goodbye, Dolley
Fare themed rooms well, Dolley
You're a slice of teacake on brash nation's lawn
Quite a bipartisan belle, Dolley
Kiss and tell, Dolley
When the Brits lit Great House, did you
Still have your Madison jammies on?

With Washington flaming
You seized portrait claiming
No intruding fuse takes our finest, founding man
So, get first lady's wrap, butler,
That's a wrap, butler
Dolley will never draw parties this way again

1818

Era of Good Feelings

The best place for war is behind us,
distant river, blood dry.

The best time for conflict was yesterday,
a pressed letter on final page, dot the i.

The best way to live with battle is without it,
treaty of peace along calm horizon, a fireproof sky.

Brits, be-gone!
America for Americans!
Let this thing called *nationalism* stretch its liberty-seeking limbs.

What transient bliss is this—
void of abiding strife,
political division!

On with Monroe, we go—
toward 1820s/20 vision.

1819

Orange Is the New Nation

What kumquat would cede Florida?

No, citrusly, what navel-head would give up all that grapefruit?

Evidently Spain.

Why, you can't swing a dead dolphin without hitting a potential sea-
port—
or route of trade!

Then again, Spain had a rainy season of reasons
to sign the Adams-Onis Treaty:

cash-strapped, indebted

unable to attract settlers (despite Florida being so a-peeling)

boundary disputes in the West

insurgencies elsewhere, in Latin America

Simón Bolívar   Simón Bolívar   Simón Bolívar

Still, the forfeiture of all that fruit and ocean front, peninsula-perplexes.

Engulfed in worldwide worries,
Spain, at least, could claim one sliver [sic] lining—

Texas.

1820

The Missouri Compromise

Building a nation is a balancing act
Divided by slavery
You cannot pick cotton
Admit Missouri with servitude.
We must draw fast line somewhere
And, as for the West,
Speaker Clay says wild prairie is

weighed upon Congressional scale.
the House debates.
walking on freedom's trail.
Admit Maine with chain immunity.
to preserve bountiful community.
why, it's anyone's guess!
a teetering territory.

Beneath parallel's belt, civil unrest—the South stirs to secede.

1821

The Saturday Evening Post

My hands are bubbled in soupy mischief.
My winsome face as innocent as a droopy pup.
Mom and Dad are barreling with anger toward flooded laundry door.
Tell Mr. Rockwell, I am ready for my close-up.

53 Market Street, Philadelphia
Its first issue, a four-page newspaper,
inspired by Benjamin Franklin's *Gazette,*
using Poor Richard's same print shop and press
to carry green society's news and tidings.

Voice of common sense, conservatism,
The Post, like any post, was urgent, honest, fresh, and informative.

Inaugural issue contained admonitions against breaking the Sabbath,
a comparative tidbit of cider versus ale, a poem about light beaming from
heaven, the coming of a solar eclipse, death of Napoleon—and, on the
back page, a new series: "Miseries of Human Life," which scorned friends
of shopkeepers from keeping customers away from counters—and such.
Ah, those were the dailies, or at least, the weeklies.

For a bicentennial of bleeds, cutlines, and features
the Pennsylvania periodical has been a mirror
reflecting the change of values, characteristics in American culture.
It chronicled footsteps of the United States across coarse continent
an assemblage of literary contributions: articles, editorials, cartoons,
poetry, humor, excerpts of fiction, non-fiction, high-quality content,
a bound hand in establishing writers.
Yes, this circular was and is a weekly, compressed, up-to-scale library,
practical, wide-minded, skeptical at sorts, moralistic,
covering everything *American* from business to etiquette
dropped at your doorstop like a bundled orphan of news,
the best friend Saturday night ever had, its tail wiggling at your shoes.

1822

Denmark Vesey's *Still I Hang*

You can swing me from swift gallows
With your triggered, twisted ties.
You can drop me like a purse of dirt.
I assure, what hangs, will rise.

Does my black bossiness inflame or cross you?
Do you suspect I'll overtake plantation, state?
'Cause I talk with fists of freedom
Pumping tongues to overcome bondage and hate.

The revolt in Haiti may indeed repeat itself,
Though history seldom lets out the same, upstart cry.
And still, I hang with fated bate-and-breath,
Though no white lung in Charleston has died.

Here beams the power of privileged rumor
In its pale, hooded disguise.
Tell all people of AME Church, it's worth all its worth.
I assure, what hangs, will rise.

1823

The Monroe Doctrine

The mastiff is among the world's most territorial of dogs.

Its *don't-tread-on-me* breed was one of few mutts aboard the *Mayflower*.

Big-boned, protective, confident and courageous when called,
the epic pooch took a lick-liking to its new backyard,
the Western Hemisphere.

And the docile creature seemed fit and fine with its master:
the companionable American citizen.

It took tooth-and-paw to digging, rolling, and discovering
the expansive property, playful prairie.

Sick of ships, weary of wars, dog-tired of treaties and treasons,
the mastiff drooled for a quiet home—
free from encroachment, puppet neighbors, crash colonies.

So, it barked at monarchs of the Old Country.
The massive canine growled at the foam of foul trade.
It panted and bayed, *Roaring empires, stay away.*

Soon, President Monroe himself was in the pound of defensive drama.
From ink written in stone, he threw Europe a deal-with-it bone.

The policy was both doctrine and dogma.

1824

Corrupt Bargain

The presidency of the United States requires a spine.

I'll scrub your back if you'll wash mine.

Speaker Clay, it's known throughout federal district:
Your political ambition is wet.
I'm reserving a stately room for you in my eloquent Cabinet.

That rogue-warrior Jackson is trouble brewing in mad west.
Why, he's a commoner, a killer, a land grubber, at furious best.

Whereas, I am fit as a waistcoat for what I'm aspiring to do.
So, why not gather your collegial electorate in favor
of good pilgrim John Q?

True. The popular vote mattered this time,
but that's all in polling past.
It's now your say that counts—the thundering *aye's*,
its spoken shadow will cast.

You name it, the keen folks of Kentucky will have it:
protective tariffs, interior roads, a derby hat full of roses—
big enough for horses to roam.

I believe this is the will (or wit) of God.
My dad John had this job.

What say you, Henry?
Revive the Congressional caucus.
Lock us into power and throne.

1825

The Erie Canal

A Wedding of the Waters,
we New Yorkers celebrate
on this auspicious autumn Day!

Along water's edge,
sycamores align, caked in gold.
A foreclosure of bank swallows swoop above boat's wake.

Come, all ye' craftsmen.
March upon ceremony's towpath—
cooper, tailor, butcher, tanner, skinner.

Down the aqueduct aisle,
it's the *Seneca Chief*
with Governor DeWitt Clinton aboard its maiden timbers.

He carries a keg of fresh water
to unite Great Lakes' pure ponds
with Atlantic's brackish tears.

Soon, goods of import,
folks of transport will embark on barges,
arrive in a fleet of new frontiers.

1826

Twology Eulogy

Lying against respective logs,
Both ex-presidents popped their clogs.

On Fourth of July, death fired some cracking kiss
Upon our nation's 50th Jubilee; how doubly ironic was this?

In time, a country grieved, at half-mast, saddened--
Still, who died first? Jefferson or Adams?

Most main streets, howbeit, held planned parades.
(Back then, news traveled at a Virginia opossum's pace.)

John's last words: "Thomas Jefferson survives."
Tom's last words: "No, doctor, nothing more. This is the Fourth of July."

Quintessential final phrases, quite--
And, at least, one dying head-of-state was right.

It took more than a jury of coroners to convince us.
This double drop was ghost of chance, mere coincidence.

In a matter of minutes, man, both bosses met their Maker,
witnessed the Southern Cross, or crucis,
Across a celebratory, sullen sky
from Monticello to Massachusetts.

1827

from Samuel Kettell's Translation of Columbus' Journal

Thursday, 11th of October; Friday, 12th of October—1492
Sea, more sea than ever witnessed on Christian voyage—
And then, evidence of land, not land itself—
Evidence in and above the proving sea—
Sandpipers, a floating green reed, bits of cane plant,
A drift-board with iron.

The crew of the *Nina* noted a branch covered with berries.

These were not baubles of the nautical world,
But things of earth's world, a new world.

Westward, the ship and two caravels carried.

Standing on the castle of stern deck, the Admiral saw a light,
A rewarding light, reflective moon, a wax-wane candle
Over what appeared steadfast ground.

The Admiral offered a silken doublet to heed-man who affirmed such claim.

Early morning, land verified, the Indians called *Guanahani,*
A bean-shaped island covered with naked people.

The Admiral went a-shore, taking Sovereign steps, prepared to speak
In the name of Our Holy Savior,
And bore the Lions and Castles, royal standard, in honor of Spain.

My captains leaped to shore to bear testimony of faith.
They proclaimed the island as footed possession for the King and Queen.

The inhabitants gathered, painted faces, the color of Canarians.
They knew nothing of arms, ignorant to blade and iron.
Some, able-bodied, swam out to the three ships. We exchanged in trade,
A pot for a parrot—a song for a servant.

1828

Tariff of Abominations

There is a certain kind of snow,

falling from Washington Capitol

upon the cotton-eyed citizens of tobacco South—

a cold, vile imposition, unwanted wind.

It has to do

with a tumultuous tariff placed on imports, British.

It has to do

with raising nullification tempers and federal revenue.

At the foot of Congress' protective pedestal,

        fret an upset brood of Southern famers, planters

who side with free trade

        who side with iron desires of Calhoun.

(And you thought it was a North/South thing—slavery

        that split the nation—

when it was more about domestic smoke stacks and foreign markets—

        Industry versus Plantation.)

1829

The Currency of Old Hickory

Andrew Jackson was dead set
against a National Bank.

The seventh president, averse
to paper money.

Still, still—

that's his bad-hair day
crowning each green and peach
$20 bill.

1830

Indian Removal Act

What pieces
sweep the human tear—
water, salt
sentiments shared
                        from a transient sea—
savage stains
trailing a river
cleansed by a change
in policy?

Docking whites
alighting Ellis Island, Castle Garden—
with fisted, manifest tendencies
require room.

Indigenous fires settle to dust—
whisked ever westward,
the strings and straws of Washington
the broom.

1831

William Lloyd Garrison's *The Liberator* & Cyrus McCormick's Reaper

The former, a newspaper,
speaks of release, *immediately,*
to all bones chattel-bound
by slavery's root-hold.

The latter, a scythe-machine,
that frees spiked wheat,
so farmers can glean
what they've grown.

A detaching idea, a swift invention—
America thinks, presses on, cog and wheel—

with an abolitionist weekly,

a handsome, horse-drawn gatherer,

both hacking archaic practices
                                        at the heels.

1832

Portrait of Chief Black Hawk

I am sitting for my portrait,
Unorganized Territory, the frame.
I won't look white flash in its thunder,
but gaze eastward, toward Lost Mississippi,
home waters, I one day will reclaim.
My cheeks are primed in oils.
My sorrows stroked in rain.

The brush is still before eponymous war.

Picture it, or paint.

Where are supports from Sioux and Winnebago?
If Ioway brothers were posed for mockery,
my model cry would die to save their names.
I know return to Illinois will lead to purchase,
but idle squat will do the same.
Sauk tongue is spitting image—extinction, I distaste.
I am sitting for my portrait,
hereafter masterpiece fitting for signature shame.

1833

Ode to Compromise

Compromise, I consider,
if not concede,
to celebrate your stable scales,
your softened sense, firm handshake
that seals the Southern tariff wails.

Nullified, the selfish acts:
threat to secede,
that denigrate our fresh nation;
brute tariff talk, set to break
our purpose at God's station.

An olive branch,
a force-bill sword,
rise and fall
like sun and moon
over our quest country
'tis of Three—
Jackson, Clay, and Calhoun.

1834

Whigs in America

Shared disdain can make a party,
cause a raucous caucus-opposition
toward the political powers that be.

Enter the Whigs,
bound by animosity,
fuming at "King Andrew,"
for his tyrannical pranks
to withdraw from a national bank,
keep South Carolina, shall we say,
state-submissive, maintained.

Caricaturing the president on a throne,
their uncrowned teeth
speaking in anti-monarchical tones,
the disgruntled Whigs are a makeshift rig—
hot-under-the-rug politicians, anti-elites—
ranting antagonists on front lawns
of their saltbox, log cabin homes—
organizing such indignation, fury—
executing the executive branch
until their snug heads make that extension—their own.

1835

Great Moon Hoax

Why wait until next millennium
to go looking for life, creatures beyond flat stars?

There must be an incredible telescope,
gullible audience around here, somewhere.

The sight, the story will be a serial submission,
one fantastic, fictive piece at a time—

deep, descriptive accounts of winged lunarians,
blue-gray tinted cousins to our bison,
traipsing the crater-plains
of a drifting moon.

For now, we will not occupy,
but observe and read them
with an eye balloon, a penny press.

The supposed discovery will not be proven by the *Sun*.
It will be published by it.

All who subscribe—believe.

Perhaps, like the Cherokee,
if we force blitzed inhabitants
                                        to move to Mars or Venus,

prints from the moon will leave
                                                a trail of cheese.

1836

Betsy Ross' Deathbed Confession

Now that my days are all sewn up,
my wish is not to keep history in stitches? *(Nurse, a glass of water, please.)*

Did I sew the first American flag?

Were those my fingers weaving 5-point cut stars
over a blue field? *(Thank you. Where's the napkin?)*

It was my shop. My upholstery business—on Arch Street
three men of most repute entered there,
a secret committee from the Continental Congress—
including Commander George Washington himself.
These astute gents of arms called upon me.
They needled me to task, put on a patriotic press.

A fresh widow, I agreed to piece the first flag,
although I was up to my apron pleats in colonial chair repair
and grief. *(Nurse? Nurse?)*

Bolts of red and white hemp cloth weren't selling well that summer,
so I decided to roll with those materials.

My mind kept seeing *Union Jack,*
but it seemed to this seamstress too derivative.
Perhaps if I uncrossed those stripes,
like the colonists uncrossed loyal hearts...there I had it, the Stars & Stripes!

Did I sew the first American flag? You bet your Betsy Ross boots I did!

Oh, I may have had a snip or two from my labor base,
chap apprentices to hold the scissors.

Severtheless, I mean nevertheless, I must take a great lap of all credit.

(Nurse, you stumblebum! Where'd she go? This dripping glass wets the bed!)

1837

Hard Times / semiT draH

Hard times
A ship sits idle in Hudson River
Reproach, blame laid on big Treasury
Depression imminent among throngs of working class

The no-notes Customs House takes only specie for payment
Indigent mother begs to straw, off her fallen feet
Mean streets are born, Panic of 1837
Even the military seems at restless repose
Something's gotta give, doubt it's the bank

Speculation has overvalued rustic, untested property
Empty pockets populate an unfair public square
Martin Van Buren assumes arduous office
Inauguration of financial issues plagues his term
Taunted effigy of past Jackson hangs in Old Glory sky

Debtors' prison swells to pressed steel bars
Ripped parachute of Safety Fund settles like agitated dust
A cracked mirror of misery reflects
Hard times

1838

Black-Eyed Susan

My feet have never broken the soil of India
My eyes are not native descendants
Of Amerigo Vespucci
I am the daughter of an unknown tribal man
Generically classified as an Indian
Politically refined as a Native American
I am the surviving member of a vanished clan

Black-Eyed Susan was my name
Though I could not keep it
I was born along the Trail of Tears
Like the wind
My father rose only to die
I buried the rhythm by his side
Where it has remained dormant for one-hundred years

Without my father, denied my mother
I left the badlands of Oklahoma
For the banks of a northern shore
A white man in Missouri claimed me
The voices of my conscience blamed me
As Black-Eyed Susan became Susan Eleanor

That was the last I saw of the wind and the rhythm
As I entered a world so foreign and dark
I played the role of society's captive
To mirror the shadows seizing my wild heart
And it was my heart's own remorse
Running like a string of unstrung horses
Striding in vain to catch a whisper
Of my family's faded cry
Unable to keep pace
Absorbed by some holy human race
Susan Eleanor lay Black-Eyed Susan down to die

Black-Eyed Susan

Black-Eyed Susan

Now, I am an old woman returning
A century out of style
Capitalism and computers
Concrete stretches
Where my unscathed spirit once roamed for miles

The call of confusion abounds
As the language is awkwardly passed around
From one acceptable term to another
Drawing blood from my veins
The Bureau of Indian Affairs attempts to legalize
Something this lawful nation may never realize
I was your sister, and now I am your brother

When my own flesh-and-blood discovered
A photograph of me last summer
Those ancient rhythms revived to dance
The orphaned wind caressed my sleep last evening
I close my eyes and dream of the chance
Of wandering down to castaway banks
Of the forgotten river
Leaving my civilized clothes on the shore
I immerse the souls of Susan Eleanor and John
And emerge as Black-Eyed Susan once more

Alongside sealed waters
A legacy of lost people awaits to embrace me
As we speak in silent tongues
We are old in nothing but wisdom
The untouched world around us is young

My feet have never broken the soil of India
My eyes are not native descendants
Of Amerigo Vespucci
I am the daughter of an unknown tribal man

1839

"OK"

Token word in our vokabulary, *OK,*
originated not in Oklahoma,
but in Massachusetts, no joke,
the *Boston Morning Post* as a stroke
of humorous pokes at a rival newspaper,
reading *o.k.* for *oll korrect*, convoking
fokes to laugh at misspelled gaffes that took
to the people like a good book—
all of this coupled with *Old Kinderhook*,
President Van Buren's nickname yoked
from his hometown in New Yook,
provoking voters and the world
who soon spoke its abbreviated
infectious gobbledygook *OK* everywhere

1840

Samuel Morse Patents the Telegraph

It is not
by dots and dashes,
as one might think,
but rather
by dits and dahs
that Morse transposed
his syncopated mode,
a curt communication
fit to transmit dispatches
via telegraph lines,
underwater cables,
wireless circuitry,
blinking lamps and lighthouses
between and beyond
a world of continents and wars.

And if you can't crack
or read the code,
you can't
..-. .. -. .. ..
- .... .
.--. --- . -- .

1841

Curse of Tippecanoe

It is with great honor and duty that I accept the presidency of the United ***ACHOO!***

Anathema. Bane. Commination. Manitou.
So many words for a curse.
Every history buff knows that the president with the longest inaugural speech
and the tersest service in office
is the same man: William Henry Harrison.
His pneumonia-induced early exit is a trivia junkie's dream.
Yep. On day 32, Old Tippecanoe bit the dusty shoe.

It appears in his younger, breath-bearing years,
our nation's 9th Commander in Chief was governor of Indiana Territory,
a leader manifest-bent and determined to snatch sacred land
from the Shawnee, part of the Five Civilized Tribes,
whose native confederacy dream died at Battle of Tippecanoe.
Tecumseh, a warrior-chief, considered the general nothing less than a thief.
The great chieftain, in flaming tongue, bedamned the man—
and future White House heads, just like him.
Beginning with Harrison, every 20 years, a president in office, will die in office.
And so commenced Tecumseh's Curse of Tippecanoe,
a solemn utterance of timely, vicennial scorn.
The hex may be about death, (speak nothing of Macbeth)
but urban legend was born.

1842

Charles Dickens Notes America

It was the best of trips. It was the worst of trips.

Approaching the summit
of his global literary sensation,
renowned author Charles Dickens
boarded the *Britannia* at Liverpool
to steam-press-sail
his hopes and theories about America.

Boston was all abuzz upon the wordsmith's arrival.
A Massachusetts mob attraction
from Tremont House to Beacon Hill drawing rooms,
Dickens himself foreshadowed
the second coming of Paul, John, George, and Ringo.

Once his pen quivered outside of New England,
however, the Inimitable's opinion of the coveted country
flipped like a pancake on a nervous skillet.

Wretched factories, pointless individualism,
scandal-seething newspapers, the hold on slavery—
all built a fumbling foundation
upon his great-expectation mind.

Why, America was as bleak as Britain,
egregious as England, louse-ridden as London—
the nascent nation already in slipshod decline.

You see.

The rappel hadn't fallen far from the debris.

1843

The Oregon Trail

Both made of hardwood,

wagon and family folk

trekked across unspoiled West

on original Oregon Trail—

fleeing and seeking

hardship, a golden new land,

a covered wheel train forming the first

American band.

1844

Peacemaker

Touted as the world's largest naval gun,
the Peacemaker was the pièce de résistance
aboard the USS *Princeton* on its ceremonial sail
down the Potomac River
to celebrate a treaty to annex the territory of Texas.

Anybody who was anybody was there,
including President Tyler and key cabinet members.

Kaboom! fired a single-shot cannon from the metal monolith.

Hooray! Encore! encouraged the sophisticated crowd
intoxicated with (gulp) afternoon delight.

Several of whom then wended their way below deck
for a toast and patriotic music.

Meanwhile, Captain Stockton loaded the massive artillery,
one more time, to discharge when passing Mount Vernon,
to honor Washington.

An anticipant lot soon gathered.

(Sometimes, it is best to let sleeping guns lie.)

This time, the Peacemaker imploded,
        hairline-fractured fatigued,
                projecting lethal hot pieces of its left side,
killing the Secretary of State, Secretary of the Navy—and four more.

President Tyler, however, was still downstairs, enjoying a wartime ditty,
belted from the lungs of his vocal son-in-law.

Saved not by a whisker, but a song.

1845

The Annexation of Texas with Addendum

(*Edgar Allan Poe publishes* The Raven, 1845.)

Though border disputes remained quite bleary,

Congress adjoined Texas into statehood series,

Over Santa Ana's dead political body—laid both nation's senate floors—

While most Americans nodded, clearly clapping,

there once came a counter-tapping—

The pound of *teponaztli* drums rap-rap-rapping—

from storied Old Mexico—they tongued of war.

"Who's that visitor," dark-horse Polk queried, "slapping at chamber door—

Tis the quest of manifest destiny, I'm sure, and nothing more."

1846

Forts

We've gotta have forts!
There's a war, there's a war going on—
one with the Mexicans, one with the Indians
crossing our borders, claiming our rivers
making our women and children
feel encroached upon.

We've gotta have forts!
Build the bastion, support the bulwark
down to each wall, rampart, and parapet—
made of limestone, adobe, whatever Mother Earth
suggests to protect.

We've gotta have forts!
At the Rio Grande, there's a boundary dispute.
Our guns high, our eyes wide, our cannons foaming at the muzzle to shoot!

We've gotta have forts!
Fort Texas or Fort Brown, Fort Sam Houston or Fort Hood!
A fortification of forts!
Cactus castles
Pueblo palaces
Why, a shielded soldier catching some shut eye \
will do that waking rifle-warrior some good.

We've gotta have forts!
With God's guard, our battlemented backs will be blessed.
First, we stand our red-dirt ground.
Then, we conquer the West!

1847

The Postage Stamp, US

Its first imprint,
a pair of philately vignettes,
with Benjamin Franklin,
George Washington
on respective stamps,
half-dime and dime.

And I wonder
if first correspondence
using the pregummed bits of paper,
the maiden mailed card—
be it jubilant or despondent—
were from Brigham Young himself,
back to fellow Mormons
in upstate New York,
Palmyra's eastern shelf—
inspired by tablets,
supported with tithes—

yes, American Moses claiming
God's pioneer-party guests
licked the Wild West,
wheeled orderly wagon train into Great Basin,
made it to Great Salt Lake City alive—
and, if so,
with how many "pap" per-capita wives?

1848

A Golden Year

With wide tin pan—
America burrows in—
Alta California, Santa Fe de Nuevo México,
a flake of gold.

Be it by treaty or pickaxe,
quilled pen or mill sacks,
the country prospects
with new borders, rare nuggets,
a broadened bear-soul.

What a glorious rush of quarry is this!
Kid California, the coolest of cowboys, saunters in—

Hasten, you fine fortune seekers,
carry a hungry shovel,
conquer both squat and incoming weaker.

Gone are temperate, Puritan days—
United States of America quickens the pace
USA!

Alongside big bank, rolling river,
the money grubbing begins.

1849

Harriet Tubman Escapes Slavery

Before I guide primary passenger,

Before I return to rail as underground help,

Before I ferry one soul to freedom's depot,

I must first conduct myself.

1850

Hot Mess

FYI—
California in "Old Spanish,"
En traducción/translation
means "Hot Furnace,"
it-ct *(in 21st-century terms)*
hot mess.

Back in ambiguous antebellum days,

it seemed like every pearl of years,
a big compromise entered (out or in):

Let's put a free state here, prop a slave state there.
Owners recover your fleet fugitives—anywhere.

From paw to pawn,
the restless bear's next plod through ponderosa pines,
Congress's next set of unsettling bills—
these random woodland maneuvers were anyone's guess.

It was, thusly, decided
to keep precious pieces divided
to continue black-and-white whip
game of chess.

1851

Sojourner Truth—*Ain't I A Woman?*

It has been a triennium, three years,
since first rapture at Seneca Falls,
initial women's rights convention—
the casting for suffrage,
a drafting of Declaration of Sentiments
for the place, position of women
in religion, society, and politics.

And if the women's movement has not come full circle,
then perhaps it has become full triangle.

In rings Sojourner Truth at a happening in Akron,
stepping up to wavering stage, the female delivers.

She speaks of white men in a bind:
women in the North, negroes in the South—
all itching to put the middling male in a fix.

Humble but hardy, Truth claims
no man need help her to a carriage, lift her over a puddle.
She can ride through the mud on her own prop and post.

She has ploughed what a man has ploughed, planted what he planted.
Eat as much, work as much, bear the beat of a lash.

She has born children into the world, just as Mary with Jesus.
When she cries for their enslaved grief,
He hears her—like the pain and prayer of any man.
God and Mary made Jesus, she insights, without earthly fellow.
So, why on Earth, cannot a woman share the same rights as man?
And if Eve flipped the world wrong, let women set it right.
Applause! Applause!
Short, but no easy speech—
and Sojourner knows women are in for long threes:
the long haul, the long climb, the long fight.

1852

The Book That Made This Great War

Anti-slavery, antebellum
Harriet Beecher Stowe's *Uncle Tom's Cabin*
or *Life Among the Lowly*
or *The Man That Was a Thing*—
the book was a kind of serial killer of southern conventions
when first published by the *National Era*
in serial installations.

The pages and passages
both unified and divided its readers
by humanizing slaves and criminalizing
the brutality, abuses of servitude, bondage.

Uncle Tom himself was portrayed
as a virtuous, Christian man,
leaning to put freedom within reach of others,
leaving his own battered soul,
strap-thrashed back—back at the plantation,
for Legree's third-degree lash and blame.

No master, no transaction could capture his true character,
the abstract absolutions washing through a man
quiet but determined, proud.

He rescued the drowning, released the exploited.

Uncle Tom took to his deathbed in spiritual silence,
dreaming of a cabin in clouds.

The novel bent the nation out of shape.
The novel whipped a country into splits, to a seething core.

(Years later Lincoln told Stowe upon first greeting—
he was shaking civil hands with renowned author
of the book that made this great war.)

1853

Liberty Bell 101

In 1752,
more than five score ago,
I arrived, in bronze tact, from London.
(Oh, right, I'm British—the sum ton of me.)

Shall we clinch and crown the obvious cliché, now?

Coming to America wasn't all it was cracked up to be.

I ruptured like a punted nut upon inaugural practice strike.

And I was there, in Philadelphia, for service, to work.
Upon repair,
I, the State House bell, dinged and donged, for assembly—
to gather lawmakers of Pensylvania together.
That's correct, *Pensylvania,* an acceptable spelling of colonial age.
I also rang to collect citizens at square to hear provincial news.

I did not become America's symbol for liberty, freedom
until my Biblical inscription from *Leviticus*
caught the awe and eye of free slaves and abolitionists in mid-19th century:
"Proclaim Liberty Throughout All the Land Unto All the Inhabitants thereof."

I cracked again at the ringing of Washington's 100-plus birthday.
I split once more when metallurgists widened that fissure to soften the blow.

Then, I fell tongue-silent, nothing to clap for,
hanging, by yoke of American elm, in bell tower of Independence Hall.

Before my now mute existence, did I tell you?
I tolled for the passing of Franklin, Washington, Hamilton, & Jefferson
when their spirits ascended liberty's one true hill.

(I must've been a good luck alarm. After all, each one made it—
dead president or sacked statesman—on a face of dollar bill.)

1854

Kansas-Nebraska Act

Outrage is like a shadow
during contentious, triggering times.

It will follow.

The Missouri Compromise of 1820 was a balanced set of wheels,
a rolling Conestoga wagon in need of no repair, whatsoever. Still,

Senator Stephen Douglas of Illinois fixed it,
repealed it, replaced it

with an act of Congress
that sent anti-slavery, pro-slavery zealots,
Free-Soilers and Border Ruffians alike
spilling into fresh territories of Kansas, Nebraska
like a broken dike

to stuff first ballot, sway last vote—for or against a coming coffle
of slaves.

Popular sovereignty was a catchphrase for its cause—
let the citizens decide with their good sense, guns, and gallows
rigged among the weeping wheatfields of vast prairie.

The whole disastrous matter was supposed to be a railroad thing—
a way to pave rails and resources to where else? California.

But North was North, and South was South—
except out West—where lawless lines were as murky as mud.

An act so self-serving and egregious,
it left America's flag wounded, flagellated
in dread, fright, and bruise

the shadow colors of blood.

1855

Walt Whitman's *Leaves of Grass*

the "barbaric yawps" of revolution, political tension, expansion,
civility, and slavery—

all come to celebrate here, rest here, cry here

in common-speak leaves of grass—

I, you, a spear of sleep, too—

the republic, democracy are entwined bedfellows—

the global atom, the gloving of Eve—

far away, there is a closeness coming,

a kindness of touch, tender arriving,

a terrestrial trinity: mind, body, & soul—the long, loaf-some soul

here the portal awaits, a patch of felt grass—

it opens, opens—

I, you, these leaves of grass—say

it opens to abide;

so, all will live and lie with us,

hillside and sound—

as revisable print on irreversible page

1856

The Know-Nothing Party

Not a blanket term
for every political party in the country
(though some disgruntled Americans may deem it so),

the Know-Nothing Party was a nativist breed,
first-born or long-resided Americans, protestants
hell-bent and dead set on curbing the influx of immigrants,
corralling the impinging Catholics,
keeping whatever is incoming to America
from power.

Fearful of Pope Pius IX's influence
atop Chair of St. Peter
enclaved some 4,000 miles away—

these ballot-driven zealots
ventured to pummel and politick
the mighty river of German, Irish fresh settlers
into a ripple of submission.

"Established inhabitants" was the platform of upstart party,
but xenophobia and loathing were not enough
to carry this secret society all the way—
to empty White House.

With its smaller factions like the Blood Tubs and Plug Uglies
bullying the poor and unprotected
in rank allies of colonial-prone cities,
the Know-Nothings soon fell into rank
with, mostly, the Republican Party—
shrouded by the issue of slavery, a nation in-waiting
for greater divide, irrepressible wound.

Know-Nothing, Whig, Democrat, Republican—
somebody better know something—and soon.

1857

Dred Scott Decision

With strike of a sound block,
I render supreme decision.

You, slave, Dred Scott,
are not a citizen of this country,
no person standing before this court
to sue.

I have not heard your plea for freedom.
Your rights, your voice
belong to an owner.

You only count among cattle,
or when head-wraps are checked
to complete a chore.

You are property that has seemed
to steal itself—placed itself here.

I will give you that.

Now, when the white man appears
to gather his chattel of things.

I, gavel, will give you back.

1858

Western Meadowlark

Flautist of flat grasslands,
whose flutter, trill whimsy
carries fair prairie
in a pod of downwind,
gurgling notes—

What flushes your wings?

Why must you fly, so godspeed and low?

Is it abrupt arrival, rise of King Cotton
upon your rangeland home?

Or a distant, but dear "House
Divided" quaking
over slavery, gold?

In a flurry of buff, brown, and white—
your sunflower breast
flees melodic, meadowy post—

with a tuft of ruffian blood
darkening the sable-scarfed "V"
beneath your throat.

1859

John Brown Just Ain't Whistling Dixie

John Brown, a white abolitionist,
is hanged for leading a slave revolt at an arsenal, Harper's Ferry, Virginia.

Daniel Decatur Emmett, a minstrel entertainer,
writes and performs the song "Dixie" in blackface at a theater in New York City, New York.

When I was young,
I thought John Brown was black,
a black slave who led a revolt
with fellow dark servants
at a plantation alongside some river
in Virginia,
yep, a militant negro,
leading an armed band of slaves
who then planned to cross blood-stained water
to perpetual freedom.

When I was young,
I thought the song "Dixie" was written—by a homesick, runaway slave
who had come across hard times in the cold North,
so far away from his family and cotton-pickin' ways.

That was before the internet,
a quick fix for accurate information.

Brown was white.
"Dixie" was a blackface tune at a white-ticket show.

(What does a 20th-century kid in the Midwest trying to pass history know?)

Perhaps, back then, all I got right:
Assumption can lead to stereotype.

1860

Civil War: More or ___

Lincoln

Elected

Southern

Secession

1861

The Siege of Fort Sumter

Citadel upon vernal sea,
acropolis of brick,
a fastness—
built and meant to be an end-all,
a bulwark, ocean-prop
to protect frond-friendly palmettos,
citizens a-shore
from perils of foreign insurgency,
mariner aggression
sailing—from an alien port.

But—*boom!* cries a sand cannon—
Here is a mortar-bullet—fired from a mad brother—

A wave of artillery, battery—
surround the undermanned fort.

Here, is an unexpected beginning,
unplanned purpose
for infernal, same-soil war.

Wrecked interior of Fort Sumter
mirrors shambled soul of America.

This must be what the confederacy of gray clouds coating
the broken blue water of Charleston Harbor is for—

1862

Bloodbath, Aftermath—Antietam

Carnage to harvest if we find enough viable men
from the rifled, the plowed.
Blood cotton to pick—
and what remains of General Lee's soldiers—gone

but not Confederacy-collapsed.

The hill-house, Dunker Church—blistered with turbulent bullets.

Whatever framework stands shall be a hospital, for now.

Clara Barton dresses the innumerable wounded with corn husks—
from blown battleground.

Downhill, the watershed, Antietam Creek flow in disarming
arteries of red.

Why, you could win a Maryland state election with the flung hands,

raised souls

of the dead.

1863

Gettysburg Address for Idiots

It's been nearly a century ago, when George Washington, Benjamin Franklin, and few other biggies back in the day, these fellows made America official by pushing papers like the *Declaration of Independence* and our *Constitution* in united spirit of 1776—that everybody here, in this free country, is equal, the same. *

Now, look what we've done. What a bloody mess! Brother fighting brother on our own soil, turning a cornfield into a battlefield, and a battlefield into a cemetery. We stand here at Gettysburg, atop, among those who died here, so that our country, somehow, someway, might become a better place once this civil disaster is over. The fallen, they deserve our prayers, our meditations.

But our being here, it will not make Gettysburg a saintly, blessed place. Only the deceased and surviving soldiers, thosc who fought and fell on this field—their memory, their legacy—will make it holy. The world will pay no attention to those of us, the living, in attendance—but will forever remember the tally, the ceaseless tolling souls of the Gettysburg dead.

As hard as this is, we, the living, must carry on during the course of this Between-the-States' war until righteous things come out of it, those things penned and promised on Pennsylvania paper—a revolution ago—freedom, equality, liberty—if anything is worth dying for, it is these three. And, then, the Gettysburg gone, they will have not died for nothing. And our nation will rise from these ashes of the war-torn and wounded, a birth of free people, all people, secure in a government built by them, to serve them—a government that provides and saves, a government that will not know the grave.

**Footnote: Everybody means everybody.*

1864

In God We Trust

If there ever were a spreadable slogan spoken, written throughout America,
this is arguably it.

Historically, a disputable phrase
of First Amendment faith
to those who contend religion should be separated
from state,
In God We Trust took the long, high road to becoming America's motto.

Literally coined by the Philadelphia Mint during the Civil War, 1864,
(with pious persuasion of Secretary of Treasury Salmon P. Chase),
the catechismal catchphrase appeared on obverse side
of two-cent bronze coin
to hoist morale, spirited sentiment to Union soldiers, supporters.

Prior to pressed inscription,
the four-word frame made its antebellum way, 1812,
into fourth stanza of Francis Scott Keys's *Defence of Fort McHenry*,
aka *Star-Spangled Banner*.

Word was, Benjamin Franklin, 1748, had an affinity for its idiom, too—
suggesting its Psalmist allusion be part of a pre-colonial militia's
colors, coronet, and plume.

In 20th-century time,
the Lincoln cent, the Mercury dime, the Jefferson nickel—
silver and gold coins, even paper currency
captured its higher-power caption, joined the trust-in-God trance.

In 1956,
out of many mottoes, US Congress chose one.

E pluribus unum never had a chance.

1865

April Tool

What indelible theater this will make!
Such lavender madness—
the downing of a dictator,
counterfeit tyrant—
for swift betterment of Rome.

I am through standing, auditioning
for bit parts to Brutus.

It is time to act, audaciously act.

A stealthy Deringer pistol in commodious pocket.
That's the ticket to calamity's gate.

Our American Cousin, the play, is the thing,
comedy-accomplice to an assassin's sting.

I must wait for audience laughter—
the vulnerability of hilarity—
a non-sensical punchline—
something about a "sockdologizing man-trap"
that will send exposed petticoats, tickled muttonchops reeling—
Lincoln's own bodyguard bent over in a belly laugh—
angled away from his post—passageway door to the President's Box.

Opportunity opens, culmination of plot.

There is the back, blind side
of the Great Emancipator's head, Tool of the North,
his inattentive limbs busy with guffaws and applause.

This single shell of lead will give death to a president,
birth to the Secret Service, the South's last spur of a chance—

I'll give it a shot.

1866

American Society for the Prevention of Cruelty to Animals

Let sleeping dogs lie.
You can't beat a dead horse.
If humans only obeyed the clichés,
there'd be no abuse to report.

Perhaps other than the acronym *USA* itself,
ASPCA was a cultural initialism of national appeal.
After all, who could hurt or hit a kitty?
What kind of knave would bruise a mule?

The idea to protect vim-and-vigor critters in this country
from the perils of distempered people
derived from, well, czarist Russia.
American diplomat Henry Bergh, appointee of Lincoln,
witnessed in wintry streets of St. Petersburg—
thwack-drubbing of horses too sapped to snap-pull a peasant cart.

Before venturing back to the States,
Bergh observed and learned from a Royal Society in London—
set in place with charter and ardor—
to capture and litigate against citizens in Swinging City
cruel to animals.

And so, began—Man's Best Friend Destiny!

At Clinton Hall, New York City,
Bergh advocated for the muted beings—
those creatures neglected,
pitted against one another for a quick bet and death,
killed in masses at slaughterhouses for consumption or pelt.

The beasts of the boroughs mattered as part of greater humane movement.
Rapacious folk were held as accountable villains.
Good for God's furred, four-legged, feathered friends.

Now, if we can only do the same for our battered children.

1867

Rejuvenalia, Goddess of Reconstruction

O, I wish
American democracy were Greek,
then we,
the collective sticker-survivors of post-Civil War,
the grateful undead,
yes, we could summon *Rejuvenalia,*
Goddess of Reconstruction,
with her tourniquet limbs,
haversack of tool-kit hair
to fix
this plantation-wreck of toasted cotton,
impasse roads of Black Codes,
the nothing that is whole in our lost landscape
of each beaten, barren home.

Drift to us,
winged and winsome *Rejuvenalia,*
Princess of the Patch,
in your fertile, myrtle gown of mending wares—
sail past candescent scalawag,
cast away that shady carpetbagger—

and with every breath

of your rarefied air—exhale

repair, repair.

1868

Due Process

Two words—
arguably, among the most important
in our *Constitution*—
they made their archival review
in the Fifth Amendment,
then resurrected
for the Fourteenth Amendment,
decades later,
to give citizenship, rights
to the newborn free slave.

Two words—
but what do they mean
in their vague, oxymoronic tandem?

It's been said that *due process*
means little or nothing to the casual citizen
unless said person sits in trouble
with stern lap of the law.

Then *due process* becomes a learning process
before one's due date in court.

If handled properly,
due process is like a fair umbrella
that protects a dry sleeve of rights on the doomiest of days—
the right to know your accuser,
the right to know the charges,
the accurate collect of evidence,
the right to an attorney,
the right to a fair and speedy trial—and so on—

Still don't get it entirely? Who does?
In spooked horse sense, *due process* pulls the reins on government
from trampling an individual into dawn's "jump-the-gun" dust.

1869

The Golden Spike

A summit
is both high point and meeting.

Here, among elevated drops of air,
scent of mountain juniper,
the associates, officers, cowcatchers
of two railroad companies,
face-to-face trains
gather in event of ceremony.

With one strike of my nugget head,
all space and time
across this nascent continent transforms
in the quickened spirit
of more civilized, expedient travel.

Each passenger, every piece of freight
become my binding business.

Driven,
each troy ounce
of my glistening verticality
presses to honor all who labored—
all who will serve and sojourn
upon these tracks and ties
of groundbreaking endeavor.

A symbol of survival,
I am California's company gift,
yet all of America's *tootin'*

buried treasure.

1870

Old Faithful

Known for its predictable temper,
steamed reliance,
the geyser is a gushing architect

of Ares' fluid rage,

untamed rain,

spurting columns
of marble smoke

out on the range

where hardy citizens wait

at a hardened-lava distance
for its impetuous intervals

to surge and spew—
do that ancient buzz, again

in mercurial, wet monuments—

Ionic, Doric, and Corinthian.

1871

Peshtigo Fire

No one murmurs about the Peshtigo Fire,
not an utterance.

Neither soul nor sparse leaf
lends an atom of oxygen
to its charred history,
intense hour—
deadliest blaze, most lethal light
in US history.

Upstate Wisconsin—*wasn't it?*
Or maybe Michigan's high peninsula,
partly in Canada?

Never mind.

All I know is that it's the Farrah Fawcett of forest fires.

You know,
the Charlie's angel who died on same June day as Michael Jackson.

Talk about coincident catastrophe.

That fire up north happened the same night,
the same October night, that Mrs. O' Leary's cow
kicked the bucket that toppled a lantern
that ignited the Great Chicago Fire,
a cosmopolitan conflagration
that consumed scores of wooden structures,
big-shouldered buildings—rendering hundreds and thousands
homeless in the Windy City.

But, where was I? Oh, yeah, Farrah Fawcett. (She had anal cancer.)
Who had time to sob over her one-piece bikini poster
when the nation was suffering in pieces to the beat of *Billie Jean?*

1872

Arbor Day

I think I'll never see a more verdant display
Than prime trees planted on inaugural Arbor Day.

The river birch, spined buckeye, the woodland ash and elm—
All rooted down to net whenever freshet overwhelms.

A million green umbrellas we crown upon Nebraska's plain
To ward from heat or cold, catch urgent plethora of rain.

With seeds of intrigue, a town newspaper plants in readers' minds
The need to rise and shovel for sake of nature and humankind.

A tree both filters and provides—
It knows whom to shelter, when to repel—when to abide.

A tree has nothing but giving—up its branch-sleeve;
And when its leafy lungs exhale, all the world breathes.

1873

Patent # 139121

America works—
on tended farm, in chip-away mines,
upon a fisted machine.

In these times of toil,
the hands of labor
often go to waist pocket
for a minute's rest, a second's shade.

R-r-r-r-i-p! Tear!
A co-worker sees your long underwear.

It's a riveting situation—
yes, riveting—and a copper one at that.

The workforce, it seems, is coming apart—
at stressed seams.

This presses Levi Strauss, a magnanimous magnate of fabric,
to partner with indebted tailor Jacob Davis
to invent, give birth to the common blue jean.

Eureka! At last, the blue jean!
Bled with indigo, tightened to a twill.
This is the durable, true California Gold Rush!
A below-the-belt staple for staff and crew—
reinforced and fast.

And for casual, or blue-collar, posterity,
this explains why *1873* is eternally tagged
on the crest of your ass.

1874

Barbed Wire: A Biography

Coined "the Devil's rope,"
the thorny fence was invented,
patented, post-Civil War—
with an iron twist—
by an innovative lid named Glidden,
as a piercing exclusion—to all encroachments,
the thorny fence's wiry monuments—
symbolizing death
of American West's wild, open, free-for-all prairie.

A shared understanding among soil holders—
framing the parameters, perimeters of tamed land,
its natural resources extinct as the dire wolf.

At first,
crops were corralled inside
the silvery spikes, double-stranded confines—
grains refrained—
from mingling with nuisance of neighboring livestock.
Dependent on waning public acres,
cattle gathered where they hoof-could—homeless on the range.

And the barbs were sharp—
arrow-dart bristles and pricks
to break the beast, leave a carcass
or careless ranch hand bleeding.

Soon, the military joined in with pointed palisades
for trenches, fortresses, castles
with strategic leaders sleeping soundly within—
their dreams knowing
anyone, anything perpetrating
this cable-laced domain would recoil a bloody limb
or—at least—go away
with a shrill of scraped skin.

1875

Aristedes

Winner of the first Kentucky Derby

He is whipping me, again,
before an encouraging crowd,
a gather of attentive hats.

It is a kind of spring flog.

The old rules say it must be this way—
this thrashing, urging—
for my heightened master's safety, support.

White-stockinged,
I can be a spooked beast,
with a tendency to run, to drift
off the scheduled plan.

Whipping. Beating.

First cringing to turn, the back stretches—

A sprig of mint garnishes the race-hastened air.

Like a hound in pursuit or purse-rabbit,
I am coursing as fast as I can.

At the end of the line,
I will be draped in a lather of sweat,
a garland of roses.

My workhorse shoulder to receive a pat of satisfaction
from this rod-and-victor, this jubilant jockey,
this keeper of the cord—

this black man.

1876

Centennial

Centennial approaches.

All Philadelphia is a world's fair.

With an emphasis in advances of industry—
Corliss Steam Engine installed at Machinery Hall,
its colossal centerpiece rises like a behemoth-battery
to expedite current air.

Centennial approaches.

Alexander Graham Bell gives America a ring.

A celebration of practical inventions—
the typewriter, sewing machine, printing presses
not to mention—first popcorn, root beer
cause a spin of tummy-springs.

Centennial approaches.

Let US count the one-hundred words and ways.

Main Hall is a near-mile wide.
Atop its transcontinental towers,
Brother Jonathan takes grand century in stride.
(With Uncle Sam creeping up from behind.)

1877

Crazy Horse

In the year of my death,
the world became a wellspring
for violence—
a chaos of Crows flying hellbent in wicked South,
steel fires in stricken East,
a frothing white foam encroaching
toward the gilded West.

I feared little. My people, the Lakota,
feared almost nothing—
except approach of the ocean,
yes, a great ocean—
that one sunset, our receding feet
                                        might fall
                                                into its bluest grave.
So, I took a stand—
a single feather defense
against the federal fury
who had broken deals, withdrawn handshakes,
seized our women, flattened our bison-skinned homes.

Once in restless captivity,
my chained frame took a bayonet in the back.
During my last breaths, I insisted to be lain on Mother's soil,
refusing to die on a medical cot.

Now, I rise and ride again,
out of mountain of carved granite,
unwounded warrior, upon my pinto Inyan,
a dark stone behind my ear—
rising and riding to memorialize the lost,
the vanished visions they quested and carried—
my unshaken hand points to sacred homeland, place
where my people are buried.

1878

Remington No. 2 Type-Writer

UPRIGHT AND OBLONG LIKE A FURNACE,

THE COLOR OF CHAR FROM A TOILING FACE,

AND WHEN YOUR PINKIE PRESSES “SHIFT,”

A CAPITAL RIFT, THE BIRTH OF lower case.

1879

Edison

I rival the night.

And like a heart pulsing
for a wild, lasting love affair,
I need something very hot—
that will not burn out.

Everything else is in place—
the glass pear-shaped frame,
dependable mount,
even a vacuum, absence of air—
so, ignited wire will not cease
to a quick sleep.

I am looking for durable material
to use as filament
to distinguish my career,
not extinguish it.

Platinum has proved, too expensive—
but this cotton, when carbonized,
acts as if it's firm treatment
to take the heat.

I rival all night—to discover an undying daylight.

A thermal thinker,
beneath a dimming reservoir of oil at Menlo Park,
I work and research with this prospect—this incandescent lamp,
this flaming Frankenstein
that, in turn, will create up-all-hours readers,
this bulbous beast
that will make city streets—albeit not secure, but safer—
with a glowing, nighttime nod to me—
and my bright tinkers.

1880

Northern Cardinal

Loud and pingy in morning birdsong
with a splashy *cheer-cheer-cheer*
its signature trill,
this pealing candy-apple breast
with eminent crest
rings like a cranberry bell.

Lovely to look at, in tow,
perched on cedar bough, dappled with Appalachian snow,
this sable-veiled prince
sits on pine like a carmine thimble.

Destined for holiday greeting card,
red-robed, raucous, its coat—war-blood scarred—
this hallmark beauty, hued in robust rhubarb,
celebrates itself as seven-state symbol—and *cymbal.*

1881

My God! What Is This?

Garfield is dead? Well, scratch my head at that!
I didn't know you could kill an animated cat.

Rest and a seaside town—
these respites would not save
President Garfield after he was railroaded
by a bullet, point-blank, in blinded spine,
another slug in left shoulder
at D.C.'s Baltimore & Potomac Station.

Assassination itself would have to be patient,
for the wounded head-of-state survived—
yes, the grave had to wait—

but only after weeks of torture, ghastly pain—
at the incompetent mitts of Dr. Bliss—
a masochistic charlatan who put the con in *convalescence.*

My God! What is this?

That was what an entourage of witnesses claimed
Garfield to say when he was stricken
by Guiteau's spitting revolver.

My God! What is this?

The moribund Preacher President also must have thought
as his vessels burst, his poisoned blood cells clotted—
when the dastardly doc's probing, tainted finger
continued to push the elusive shot of lead
closer to dying chief's pancreas and liver,
closer to heaven's waiting stair—
with Clara Barton and the newfound Red Cross
fighting a fire with clean prints and pints of blood—at Michigan's Thumb—
a devastation elsewhere.

1882

Quiet Spikes

Softly, we set
our bamboo coolie hats
on a blanket of high Sierra snow.

Segregated, tacit, and tired,
a bundle of fallen pine cones as common fire—
we huddle for heat
as white laborers nestle in woolen quilts
upon downy village, below.

Our loose-fitting muslin shirts, soiled trousers—
they serve as pajamas.

In dreams,
we build ceaseless tunnels and tracks,
then our helpless, helping hands disappear—
by federal act.

No more of our Chinese brothers to come.

All rail work is done.
We blasted last mountain with a spike of nitroglycerine—
enough to give heaven—a hole.

It cost six fingers, four limbs,
both yin-and-yang souls.

1883

Pendleton Act

This should bring an end
to ruin of the spoils system,
a finality to friendly favors,
relative fraud,
dubious appointments
routinely dispensed
by elected, seated officials
those ministers of power
who practice cronyism,
nepotism that unlawfully
shower the unmerited, incompetent
with patronage, a job,
salaried security,
a place in public service—
most ill-gotten—
for lending their support
to victory for the greasy Big Cheese,
even though his entire political machine
smells rotten.

1884

Mudslinging

Ma, ma, where's my pa?
Gone to the White House—ha, ha, ha.

Like an unwashed piece
of thrift cloth,
it is old and dirty—
and best to avoid altogether
if you can avert its hideous hurl.

Its smeary heaves have been around
since the late 18th-century elections,
when Hamilton accused Jefferson
of sleeping with slaves.

Leave it to American politics
to turn the tongue into a no-relief pitcher.
The "Dodger" election of 1884 was no exception—
with to-and-fro mucky throws
ranging from a bastard child—
to Mulligan letters proving a series of big-business bribes.

Allegedly,
Democrat Grover Cleveland fathered a son out of wedlock.

Purportedly,
Republican James Blaine was tattooed with "Rum, Romanism, & Rebellion."

An assault of invectives cropped up in the guise of damning questions.

Did Cleveland eschew service in the Civil War?
Has Blaine been in deep pockets of Congress for sake of railway tycoons?

Campaign and stain. Stain and campaign.

That stubborn spot won't be coming out soon.

1885

Washington Monument Dedication

A
few
words
to dedicate
this column
mineral pillar
pointed ray to
high heaven
an obelisk of
bluest gneiss
white marble
upon fair plain
pearl monolith
that honors a
man of firsts
first in camp
first in office
agile general
fit president
who set firm
a foundation
on this land
in our hearts
a man whose
august faith
grit courage
places him no
less than first
in our nation
a man who's
earned this
slendersalute
standingstone
OVATION

1886

Statue of Liberty Enlightens, Unloads on You

Lady Lagniappe,
I am a gift from France—
to celebrate America's centenary, reciprocal support,
cessation of war.

My given name is *La Liberté Éclairant Le Monde,*
Liberty Enlightening the World

One might say *Statue of Liberty* is a favored sobriquet.

A decade in design,
I did not exactly ship overnight,
though my right arm, clutching a torch
preceded the rest of me.

Packed in crates,
aboard the French frigate *Isère,*
my Eiffel spine and I
sailed the sea with its salt air—
the first to green my copper creases.

And when, at last—
this austere *ballerine*-in-boxes arrived
if I may apprise,
like the immigrant,
I came to this country
in pieces.

1887

Groundhog Grief

What haven't I weathered?

Each year, it happens—
second sunrise of February—
the paunchy men of Punxsutawney
handsy throbs of Gobbler's Nob
gather in dark coats,
pompous top hats
to extricate my frightened fur
from this climate-controlled,
tourist-trap zoo.

It is a forecast, they want—
a prognostication—the waiting nation desires.

These pawing men of noted Inner Circle,
this maddening morning crowd—neither troop disturbs my sleep.

Awake for the ages,
I do not hibernate.
I do not hunt, dig, or live—as other woodchucks do.

At once,
I am hoisted into the networked air,
displayed like the lake sturgeon, catch-of-the-day,
then placed on a blood-carpeted stump
in the company of rodent-written, pun-hungry scrolls.

Hear ye! Hear ye! What have I seen?
A shadow of a man
with his pathetic club-cronies
who all need to get a shave and a life
from top to bottom.
To hell with winter and spring—I'm heading back to my burrow
to dream of summer and autumn.

1888

There's No Business Like Snow Business

Irving Berlin was born this year—off, off Broadway—in Siberia,
of all places, the Russian Empire. Siberia—where winter never sleeps.

I once thought Irving Berlin was birthed in, well, Berlin.
And if not Berlin, then New York City, the Big Apple,
which, by the way, grappled with the Great Blizzard of '88
in its own shivering, drift-smitten, igloo-infrastructure way.

Berlin and his Jewish persecuted family would immigrate here
a few years later—after the paths had been cleared
for safe pedestrian passage—and fame.

Face it. The kid knew wicked weather.
Upon his arrival, I wonder if young Israel Beilin, Irving's real name,
gathered in his head, past pictures of frosted Gotham in a vice grip of ice,
folks huddled frost-bitten cheek to cheek,
its citizens transformed, transfixed into makeshift architects
of snow tunnels and mitten-packed caves. *Grammy, get your shovel.*

Did Berlin catch the photograph of that abominable patch in Central Park?
Or the Broadway marquees teeming white with frigid foam?
Who showed the songwriting sprite
scrapbook evidence of the drift dumpster in Brooklyn Heights-
where brownstones became *b-r-r-r-ownstones?*

And at sea, New York Harbor—grimacing images—
                        a frozen foundering with white-out waves—
                pirating plates of ice, tumbling-dice crystals
ship decks wickedly slick and anchored by high, ravenous winds,
                their imperiled yaws caught, ravaged
        bobbing in a scant-blue typhoon
                        sinking in a snowstorm
of tempest-tugged boats, battered-blind galleons
with not a sailor's soul left to witness aboard the USS *White Christmas.*

1889

Omnibus Bill

When I was in third grade,
I missed the word *omnibus*
on the basic skills' test
we children in Iowa had to take each year,
and the rest of standardized-student nation, for that matter.

I thought omnibus was some kind of bus,
a double-decker one, maybe,
with *omni* aboard it—
whom I supposed were a type of Eskimo—
a bus load of Eskimo. That's it!

Wrong.
It seems that *omnibus* is a word for something that covers, well, everything,
like the previous sentence of this page.

Legislators *ya-ing* and *nay-ing* beneath gilded domes like to use it.

Take 1889, for example—
the territories of the Dakotas, Montana, and Washington—
all became states in one enabling Congressional swoop of approval.
The Dakotas split—North and South—
due to population differences, railway connections, lifestyles
of the poor and blameless.

Yep, four new states rubber-stamped then admitted by a single bill.

My guess is that most Americans back then,
from the Butte ranch hand to ingénue Wall Street tycoon,
at least understood it,
not like the complex omnibus bills—these days—
that stack trillion-dollar budgets with earmarks and pork packages
that no ordinary citizen could ever decipher.
Why, it's enough to darken the doorstep on a clear, new day—
but, at least, the US West became wider (and whiter).

1890

Coda of the American Frontier

Perhaps the last passenger pigeon
in its final flight, swan song, across bounded continent
could croak of the wilderness' demise,
the end of its uncomposed composition—best.

It's settled then.

Indeed, the slate-gray bellwether of extinction
might bird-speak for all fauna and flora
that unceremoniously closed at close
of the American frontier—
the prairie dog, Labrador duck,
the Franklin tree, mariposa lily—

the ghost wing of the passenger pigeon,
once abundant, a plethora of pecks
in limitless integers upon a free-range sky—

Its tendency to flock in masses made it a serene target, simple quarry
for shotguns populating and popping the open fields
for leisure and meat.

Swift, graceful, gregarious bird—
outmaneuvered by tracts, encroachments, counts of the Census Bureau
with its tallies and triggers.

At rest in a circle of crosshairs, the passenger pigeon—

if it were alive today, it would twitter.

1891

Opening Night at Carnegie Hall

Tchaikovsky was there,
and the Russian composer was supposed
to debut a new orchestral work
for festive May occasion.

Instead,
the maestro from Moscow
conducted his *Festival Coronation March,*
(rechristened as *Marche solennelle*),
a piece commissioned for Tsar Alexander III
some eight years prior.

A better part
of the cultured tympanic membranes seated in Music Hall
got woodwind of, identified the original music in D major.

The dubious visiting director was caught in tap act.

Its notable tune even suspected, recognized
by a guild of parquet ushers.

No matter—applause resonated the mahogany hardwood floor
of the Mid-Manhattan concert venue
like a command-performance canyon—

which only proved, Pyotr, you duplicitous goose,

Americans were more familiar with your oeuvre
than the Russians.

1892

Pledge of Allegiance

Nearly fifty syllables: just one adjective-indivisible

Bound for quoted fame,
delivered each morning
like a bottle of fresh milk,
this pithy promise to our country
first appeared in a Boston youth magazine
to commemorate the 400-year sail
of Columbus.

Initially dispatched
as a kind of military salute,
the proper etiquette, stance refined
to where solemn right hand
discovers the heart's chambers.

In reverent, recited applause,
the little ones vow daily cause—
before sitting down to be schooled
of history's lethal dross:
two world wars, Hitler, communism—
hellish threats,
sound reasons why the phrase
"under God"
appended to "one nation"
half-a-century later.

1893

America the Beautiful in Peak Draft

Imperial feast for the eyes,
this infinite prospect, boundless panorama—
my gaze atop Pikes Peak
effects a summit
for my breathless soul.

Diction, Katharine, *diction!*
Every fertile piece of plain,
each tawny tide of grain
must receive, deserve to be given
the proper adjective, right word.

And the peaceful, wide sky—
it is both *halcyon* and *spacious,*
I think I'll go with alliteration here—
spacious sky, no, *spacious skies.*
The clouds above
this glorious range hang
anything but lonely.

My visiting professor voice,
it longs to cry out like a robust roll call—
echoing, along and across the weathered canyon—
America! America!

And these kingly stones,
magnanimous mountains
in stately quietude
occupying seats of vast dominion, below,
there *must be* a color
for their regal mingle of dark red, deep blue circles—
plum, lush lavender?

Oh, I'm sure it will come to me
from a coach window on the train ride, home.

1894

Labor Pains

We could all use a day off,
a grinding halt to frenzied workweek itself—
a time to breathe extended leisure of air—
put a herd of beef patties on spitfire grill—
watch a once green leaf
earth-tone ease into yellow, ochre, or crimson.

September rings the recess bell for me.

Why, I was working, feeling the heat all summer—
a spot welder for the Pullman Railway Sleeping Car Company—
until ardent strike broke out, South Chicago,
in a bloody band of protest.

It didn't take no midtown math-man
to figure out what nickel-and-dime cruelty was accruing.
The Gilded Age had stiffened to an overexpanded crust.
Panic followed like snakes to an Irish flute.
Our wages were lowered like a dead man's coffin.
But our rents in Pullman were maintained, simmering
like a quivering lid of potted steam.

It blew. We blew. The nation's mail screeched to a standstill....
It was first-class disaster.
Boycotts broke out like a ginger kid's acne.
Rail cars tipped over like napping heifers.
Federal troops blew in to quell prairie pandemonium.
In the blood-bath aftermath,
dozens of railroad dissidents, union-pushman fists, killed or injured.
To placate public outcry,
President Grover Cleveland proclaimed
an immediate Labor Day—moving it from May to September—

The misses, kids, and I are packing our picnic to set foot to Jackson Park—
but nearby cemetery, fall's Memorial Day, that's where memory enters.

1895

Cast Down Your Bucket Where You Are

After Booker T. Washington's Atlanta Compromise Speech

Here is a ship
of former slaves,
free to challenge abrupt waves
encountered on a southern sea.

Its cargo, for the moment, sails
without fresh water.

This is an obvious, pressing need.

There are other boats inhabiting this mist—
this pelagic plantation—
hulls of alabaster that have reaped
great quantity and reward
through experience, pain, and grit.

Ashore, await great riches, high position,
boundless amounts of pristine drink—
but all of that is at an endless distance,
an unattainable tomorrow
unless you raise the sole bucket
at your dehydrated heel—
then cast its thirsty lid down, here and now,
toward your neighbor fluidly afloat
at your port side.

Ashore, opportunity watches.
In its arms, infant business and upstart farms—
waiting to be tended by good mates
aboard both masts
sailing the final nautical mile
quenched and delivered
from the turbulent marine, unmarred.

1896

Plessy

He was 7/8s white,
could've been your Caucasian cousin,
but even one drop of blood made you black
in the post-Reconstruction South,
once daunting federal troops withdrew.

A humble, dutiful shoemaker,
he was headed home
from a day's work in the French Quarter,
bought himself a first-class ticket
at the Press Street Depot,
aboard the East Louisiana Railroad,
which, in turn, took him all the way to the Supreme Court—
free of charge, but not free of cost.

A Negro in first class—
well, they couldn't have that—
the train's wheels broke to a militant stop.

The affronted conductor confronted Homer—
with a Hobson's decision—
Either get back to the colored car,
or get off.

Plessy refused, then arrested
each *separate-but-equal* gavel contested.
After all, what did a bothered cobbler have to lose?

It's difficult for the passenger eye to see
the snowdrops falling from the bayou's silverbell tree
when you're face-down and shamed in a rattling caboose.

1897

The Patriotic Piccolo

I wish I were more musically inclined
to describe, specify its piquant ascent
its dotted climb.

In Sousa's *Stars & Stripes,*
of which I forever speak,
I am most impressed
by this silver twig's
breaking leaps.

A sparking shoot, fleeting motif
its thrush-like timbre
tops all top brass
at march's last trio release.

With winsome retelling
of all woodwind melodies,
this airborne cricket
rubs it darting wings.

This nimble needle,
whistle-stopper of shows,
the smallest of songbirds
lofts inside the nation's heart—
lifts solemn chambers
to a soaring state,
with heightened octave
of its own.

1898

Give Me Some Sugar

Not many wars involving
the *here-here* of ocean-split hemispheres
begin and end
in the same calendar year—
but this, the Spanish-American War, did.

Cuba wanted out of Spain,
which, since the Atlantic divided both terrains,
seemed plausible.

The US had invested millions
in Cuba's profit-prince industry, sugar cane—
and, when something like a mine, or lie,
blew up the USS *Maine* in Havana Harbor—
a world-wide skirmish at sea launched
like a wave of amphibious cannon at Naval ready.

Like a cigar without an oxidizing agent,
Spain was no match.

In the Philippines alone,
the Spanish armada at Manila Bay was popped
to smithereens.

Guam, Puerto Rico, and Hawaii became precious island possessions.

My! That was molasses gathered quick.
And what a collection of Pacific seashells to add to American pick—
which leads to one final, crystal-clear claim.

The cane of Spain lies mainly on the Cuban plain.
(By George, I think the US has got it!)

1899

Yellow Journalism

The color of canary, this just-released news,
so close to corruption—so far from the truth.

The flaxen phrase originated,
where else, from New York City newspapers—
two publishing heavyweights—
Joseph Pulitzer's *World*
and William Randolph Hearst's *Journal*
duking out dollars to win
the prize cartoon character "Yellow Kid,"

locking headline horns
with hyperbolic haymakers
to sell the most penny prints to Queens
and her brother boroughs.

Fiction blended with fact like bitters and bourbon
in an Old Fashioned.

Mock pieces of fallacious sensationalism—
all speciously edited and "misproofed"—
to turn a competitive coin.

AMERICAN TROOPS STOOP TO TEAR DOWN CHINA'S GREAT WALL!

HURRICANE RIPS THE 'NORTH' OFF OF NORTH CAROLINA!

USS *MAINE* BOMBED BY SPAIN, VANISHES IN BLOODIED HARBOR!

ROVING POLITICIAN UNCOVERED WITH VAUDEVILLE STRIPPER!

The junk-hungry customers bought it,
lined up at the stand-stoop like pigeons for bread.

(Just don't expect the striking Newsies to deliver.)

1900

Vignette for the Fin-de-Siècle

With her mother's pilfered knitting
scissors, a bored Victorian girl
operates on her German-imported
Heinrich Handwerck doll.
Its bisque head and limbs
liberate, roll away,
wheel into the twentieth century
like a Panzerwagen.

1901

The Assassination of Robert Todd Lincoln, in Triplicate

Death surrounds me
like locomotives at the Baltimore & Ohio Roundhouse.
With two cherub brothers dead, and another's (Tad) impending,
I kneeled in grief, bedside, Petersen House,
as my father bounded to darkness.

If that was not enough, I was an eyewitness to Garfield being shot.
Serving as Secretary of War,
I stood behind my Cabinet boss at DC station.
All about me departed, down.
My God, the sorrows I had wept in that town.

With my mother, Mary, mad and gone,
I took to corporate rails; but not for long,
when, on a train to meet McKinley in New York,
I was apprised an anarchist struck him, point-blank, in upper cork.
Incoming me, RIP, all aboard.

1902

Teddy Bear

Forbearance, if one's inclined to puns,
yes, rough-rider restraint was precisely
what President Theodore Roosevelt exhibited
when offered by his Mississippi wilderness guide
a small black bear, a practical cub,
roped to a willow tree like a palomino at a livery stable.

At close range, a simple shot—
why, all other hunters on the governor's expedition
had gotten their ursine lot,
but Telescope Teddy
put his Winchester stock in steady dirt, gazed away,
while vaulting his halting left hand
in rote refusal to slay such a facile, furry target.

A Washington *Post* cartoonist caught city-wind
of the Colonel's sportsmanlike, tender-timber gesture.
(Berryman was the name who lampooned
the pince-nez Executive's fair-chase endeavor.)

The newspaper's readers, all of the Eastern seaboard—
so endeared by the President's noble control,
a candy shop owner in Brooklyn decided to stuff
a symbolic, sewn bear to sell for cuddles and show—
so, *Bully! for Teddy!* and the sensation-creation
of the teddy bear in the, then, struggling toy market—
and for giving us something to cling to at night—
besides the predictable pillow (and the volatile husband or wife).

1903

Kitty Hawk

Here, by land and sea, my brother,
we take to air—

1903—the world is a runway before us.

From bicycles, kites, to gliders,
good partner—
we team with first bird, prime Flying Machine;
we teem like this fitful, sidekick ocean
with rolling ambition.

This ponderous craft sits within
our power and control to sustain—roll, pitch, and yaw
among benevolent winds, witnessing dunes.

Success needs only a fleet moment;
it is failure that requires forever.

True. We have waded in data of doubt.
The lift of the early century has oft dragged
upon down wings, shiftless wings.

December draft is clear for test engineers.

With invention's motor and propeller, Wilbur,
a handful of seconds is all we require
to create maiden stage, infant aviation
for remains of freighted history.

My heart is taking off, guiding me—fly it, fly it.

When craft and my carried soul return to earth,
so will birth

of plane and pilot.

1904

The Scoop on Invention of the Ice Cream Cone

Or should I say, *Dish.*

Rumor serves—
it might have happened
at the St. Louis World's Fair,
when a popular vendor
simply ran out of dishes—
or, at least, clean ones.

Quite a pity, on a sweltering summer's day
with all the globe in Olympic-size line
for a chance to lick Napoleon,
I mean, spoon Neapolitan.

In adjacent booth,
a Syrian concessionaire, Ernest Hamwi,
noticed the paucity of plates
available to place beneath
the flavorful bulbs of cream.
Instead of closing up the silk-candy shop,
he had a batter idea:
his waffle cookie.

This confection could be shaped into a cone
before completely cooled—
no wares to wash, no tummies to turn away,
treat-depleted.

Matter settled.

The Modern Games were simultaneously in play
at that foundry-town's other stage.
I say, if we can't give Hamwi first patent—
at least dip him some credit for crater-creating
something yum-crunchy for our competitive planet.

1905

Let Las Vegas Run

Water, when given
a piker's chance
to run,
is a predatory bird.

Why, its cuckoo's course
can devour
a snapper-in-sand catch
like the Mojave Desert
in one oasis—flat.

With a mountain's blessing—
water, that blue-crested,
white-tailed, thirsty-dirt sprinter
will carve through a spot meadow
like a wily knife—

and when its intrepid head
rushes upon a railroad
at abandoned fort depot,
well, *Dynamite!*

It will marquee-mate for life.

1906

San Francisco Earthquake

It is these souvenir looters—
many of them businessmen bedecked
in derby, bowler, and trilby hats—
who impede the military,
Presidio soldiers from channeling through
the hoard of rubble, upstart fires, miasmic heap of debris.

Dedicated troops of rescue, hindered,
by a cinder-and-ash roadblock of tailored vultures—

the city's own merchants and traders,
dressed in dark coats, fit in custom pants
for a Wednesday's morning exchange—
who are combing through wrecked kitchens,
crumbled mantels—looking
for untethered treasures, or a gimcrack to claim.

1907

Typhoid Mary

What doolally is this!
Crass balderdash, I tell you!
Quarantining me—
a busy cook, healthy woman.

Why, I am as fit as a spit of pasta
on a slotted spoon.

Blaming me—
as a carrier of contagion, disease
like a cattle tick or circus flea.

And that damned sanitary engineer,
paid by city taxes, no doubt,
to chase me for my test-tube legs,
to put my frame in a Petri-dish bed,
to make me a scorned specimen
as my final career.

Thcsc lcmon-skinncd Bronx papcrs
standing firm
on columns of lampoon and libel,
they doodle and tell.
Their fat publishers should pay me
a fatter salary for baneful slander they sell.

Me elbows know the way around soap and water.
I washed me fists and fingers, raw and rosy,
before serving the rich peaches and ice cream.

But there is no use crying the Celtic Sea
over this spilled kettle.

Pure salt and boilers could not make
this tainted tank of noodles from being unclean.

1908

Ford Model T

Built like a barouche carriage
missing a span of horses,
a suppress of reins—
this boxy, crest-heavy contraption
paved the route to road accessibility,
vehicular ownership for anyone
with one pocketful of everyman's dollars,
another filled with wanderlust dreams.

A mother of a car,
Tin Lizzie birthed a brood of contributions
to the way the nation moved and meandered.

Audacious automobile,
fitted and firmed at a Detroit assembly line,
where the workers remained stationary
while bit parts traveled by,
the cranked heap of steel and wood
put the country on easy street,
connected the prohibitive trails
of country and town.

The word *drive* suddenly received
a plenitude of lovely phrases—
Sunday drive, leisurely drive, family drive
with the misses and kids—
who were *beware-aware* of precarious gas tank
beneath the passenger seat
situated like a fuming picnic basket.

Everyone kept a lookout for bumps
and the fussy mother-in-law
bunched between feuding children
upon the backseat church pew—
in case she blew a gasket.

1909

My Life as a Prairie Dog

Like the human heart,
I rely, survive in chambers.

The burrows I dig
provide sunken sanctuaries for food, air, shelter—
mythic irrigation.

The work is intricate,
close-knit,
like my coterie, or family of other pups,
the barking squirrels that live with me
in our part of underground town.

Homesteading made me a pest—
a nuisance to the herds of humans
who wanted the grasslands their navigable way.

Flat houses from Kansas fell upon me
like plotted debris from a wizard's tornado.

A keystone species,
virtuous and altruistic,
I till myself out, then delve back in.
I share what is still there, there
with the black-footed ferret, mountain plover.

Diligent herbivore,
I clip vegetation to see what predator,
or progress is coming
that might contribute to my continued undoing,
that will leave my short-armed legacy:
a rodent in ruins.

1910

Sizzling Symbols: Boy Scouts of America

Illuminated with emissions
of spurting gold,
the Boy Scouts of America trefoil,
threefold,
points to duties
to God, others, self
like an ambitious arrow
or a crying-out-loud candle.

Build a fire.
Pitch a tent.
(That's where the oath to innocence went.)

Daybreak's ashes and anguish
simmer down
in snuffed scandal.

1911

Triangle Shirtwaist Factory Fire

Fiasco must have partnered, kindled
with not-yet-coined Murphy's Law
that unfortunate Saturday afternoon
on the 8th floor of terracotta-framed Asch Building
in Greenwich Village.

Factory women, many of them girls,
immigrant Jews and Italians,
rushed to their deadly demise
once a flick of a supervisor's fat cigar
lit a scrap bin.

Everything that could go wrong—went wrong.

Mistrust.
Fire exit doors were locked as a means to deter employee theft.
Seamstresses leaving for the day had to be inspected in long lines
for stolen strings of thread, cloth pieces.

Unsupportable Rust.
The lone fire escape twisted, collapsed under weight of the frenzied, fleeing.

Flammable Fabric
The spring season meant light-cotton textiles hanging on paper hangers,
dressed to dance with fire at first invitation of ignition.

Stubby Ladders
Rungs of the New York City Fire Department reached only to 6th floor,
tempting the upper-floor, trapped, garment gals to jump and catch a rundle.

Flimsy Nets
The jumping sheets were no canvassed match for the anvils of gravity
falling from the smoky blacksmith sky.

Triangle Shirtwaist Factory Fire

Poof! Went the Fireproof.

The clay-based exterior
designed to protect the building's façade
provided no shield to the interior's blazing intrusions.

In smoke-swept aftermath,
a needless employee butchery,
matinee bloodbath,
senseless, combustible swarm.

In fruitless gush of wet hoses,
a word to head honchos—
safe and dry in gilded Manhattan townhomes—

reform, reform.

1912

A Partial Colossus

After Emma Lazarus' THE NEW COLOSSUS

Titanic was to consort with my torch,
bring to me her tiered wealthy, pugnacious poor,
heralded masses from celebrated sea,
not these numbed-and-stunned fractions,
stiff-hinged refugees, blanketed survivors,
one for every two deceased,
without pride, without purse,
continental refuse of Poseidon's curse.

Beneath my heft of liberty,
they still appear homeless, tempest-tossed,
cataclysmically incomplete to me.

It is not nice to beguile the Mother of Exiles.
Grieved, I crack the light on this forlorn golden door.
My gift, my lamp moves along a blue, paralytic shore.

1913

The Imposition

Come on, America!
Let's do The Imposition.
A federal income tax—
Uncle Sam passes the mandated hat.

You put a dollar in.
You pull 86 cents out.
You wonder where your wages went.
Nickels and dimes scatter all around.

This levy is a heavy.
Only death will kick it off its mound.
That's what the 16th Amendment is all about.
Clap! Clap!

1914

USS *Neutrality*

Neutrality is a vessel
President Wilson christened
to appease
early-warbird Serbs,
to placate
Austro-Hungarian feathers
irked by pistol-clipped rebuke
of the Archduke—
a policy-liner from The Professor
sure to surge unbiased steam,
full-hull, ahead,
without favor, without fail;
but when crafty German U-boats,
with stalking periscopes
commenced to torpedo
domestic merchant floats,
Woodrow himself had to profess—
his evenhanded keel,
disinterested ship
simply would not sail.

1915

My First Home Run

I wish my mom, Kate, was here to see it—
my first trip around the sawdust bags
in the major leagues.

My hefty bat slugged Warhop's underhand slant
like an unwanted housefly at a family picnic.

I hit that ball of yarn to high heaven,
high in right field of the Bronx Polo Grounds,
high enough for Mom, my fistful of deceased siblings
to see.

When I stand at that plate,
I pound, but not at some incoming pitch.

I pound at the past—
a tough kid's nights in Baltimore on rainy, waterfront streets,
fighting a few punks
over nickels, or name-calling.

By George, I pound for George, my dad—
working overtime, pushing beers, tending bar at his own saloon.

I pound the life into my stillborn sisters and brothers.

I pound each cough of consumption
that rendered our mother sickly,
left me a "thought-orphan," delinquent boy in city dirt.

I pound that imminent, stitched intruder—wayward, wall-ward,
too see how it likes it—to be out there, spinning, tossing,
on your own.

I pound for the upper tier—to catch my mother's fallen tear—
and wherever baseball takes me—I'm always coming home.

1916

They Lynch Elephants, Don't They?

A menagerie of circus critters,
among them, Mary the Elephant,
marching in trunk tandem,
down Moonlit Road, in Appalachia,
one late, leaf-bearing day.

When the tusked star
of Sparks World Famous Shows
detects a rind of roadside watermelon
with her sensitive trunk,
all pachyderm-calamity gives way.

In preventive measure,
her ingénue handler
(just yesterday, a bellhop)
beats the fruit-seeker with a metal hook
behind a delicate ear.

That's a wrap for such a raw rider.
With a clutch and a coil,
the torched herbivore flings the doomed-removed beside her,
then stomps on his head with mad-mammoth foot.
All paradegoers stampede away in witness fear.

The mushed man bursts,
well, like a watermelon.
Mary the Elephant is cried and claimed
a murderous, bloody street felon;
but no bullets, no electrical charge will extinct her.

In neighboring town, Erwin, Tennessee,
there is this here railroad derrick box car,
with a Jumbo crane to pull that perilous beast
to a herd of hanging sanctuary stars.
That will show that showstopper. That will trumpets-away teach her.

1917

Doughboy's Lament

How can I refuse him,
the red tie, white goatee, blue swallow-tail coat?

His imperative trigger-finger points,
protrudes out of the recruiting poster
like an insistent ballistic.

He is pledge and allegiance—amplified, personified.

His clouds of lowered brow remind me of my father.

Signing my draft card is reminiscent
of voting a ballot for Wilson.

What was the president's triumphant slogan?
Oh, yes—*He kept us out of the war.*

Europe will be chilly.

The US Army dresses us, the selected, in limbs of wool.

My chest is a bandoleer of coveted grenades.

Trench boots of chrome cowhide
offset the softness of my overseas cap.

With haversack, canteen, cartridge belt, rifle, and bayonet,
I am check-listed, equipped to fight for Uncle Sam's flag.

You'd think my heart would be pumping cherry-to-the-ready,
but through my inner-order rolls
a kind of olive drab.

1918

Fourteen Points

First, no secrets, not a classified pact
The seas guaranteed free for world-wave trade
Equal commerce for countries true to fact
Nations lay down all arms, except safe-grade

An end to empires, inhabitants rule
Leave Russia to Russia to guide herself
A Belgium restored to its pre-war jewel
Return of Alsace-Lorraine to French shelf

Italian frontiers brought to clear borders
Austria-Hungary free to dissolve
Balkan nations accorded fit order
Turkey in place, with strait access resolved

Poland's pass-entry to brisk Baltic Sea
Birth of guild of nations to build world peace

1919

The Progressive Paradox

The thought of my wife
receiving the right to vote
is driving me to drink;
but it's illegal
for me to imbibe,
and that's the rub.

Why, just last year,
she couldn't cast a ballot
for the milkman,
yet I could consume my booze
in private or pub.

This is social justice—*phooey!*

The misses gets to drop a straw
for the next president—
while I have to draw my gin
from our bathtub.

1920

Roar, Roar, Roar

It marches in with a post-war roar—
a rumble, a shout, barrage, and a blast.

The bee's knees are buzzing cities.
The cat's pajamas are Satchmo and Jazz.

What a windfall time for women—
the flapper, silent actress, bluestocking suffragette.

The consumer takes over culture, the big cheese
with off-the-rack outfits, armoire refrigerators, wrapped cigarettes.

KDKA from Pittsburgh waves frequent air
with first radio broadcast.

Prohibition bans liquor,
but such dry discouragement will not last.

At the Cotton Club or some juice joint,
spiffy heels dance the Charleston, the Waltz, the Tango, the Fox Trot.

The bopping owls call out for more boogie—
until a fire extinguisher calls for collared cops.

Sulphur Springs, Art Deco spiraling, long-distance dials will cost a pocket,
so, buddy, you better carry a bucket of clams.

Yes, the 1920s marches in with a post-war roar—
(stumbles out with a market crash).

1921

Quiet on the Set

If you film
America's first movie queen,
Mary Pickford as Little Lord Fauntleroy
in a rags-to-riches
sequence of dreams,
do it in silence.

If you cast
Chaplin as the Tramp,
taking in a note-clad orphan,
teaching tote-lad to throw stones,
so vagrant-glazier can repair splintered glass,
do it in silence.

If you massacre
a Tulsa load of coloreds without reason or sense,
burn their Oklahoma homes
to a post-riot, red-dirt of ruins,
leave innocent victims to winter in shivering tents,
do it in silence.

1922

Lincoln Memorial

If you climb
four score and seven steps
to where I am seated,
like democracy itself,
inside this Parthenon
along swift Potomac River,
you will see and perceive,
my true meanings
in both hands—
one clenched—resolute and determined
the other—open and free.

The is the dichotomy
required of any presidency—
firm and amenable,
flexible, but strong
to abide, navigate
the currents that run through our country—
seeking peace and unity.

A colonnade of marble pillars
serve as backbone
to this commemorative cast
of inaugural walls,
addressed words—imperishable principles
upon such impressionable stones.

A bronze pall falls
from lofted girders
for war bereaved and buried.

At midnight,
it is tourist-rumored,
I gleam like a penny.

1923

Hubble Discovers a Next-Door Neighbor

This telescope is Pegasus,
my magnificent, winged horse.

It will fly me through the known universe,
take me to Andromeda.

The beast's mirroring kicks
will light and lead us

to a fantastic possibility,
a fresh-goddess, galaxy-like muse

with nova-like stars
of her own.

When Andromeda's spiral island-universe winks,
a resolution, no, a revelation

breaks through a nebulous existence:
what was once premised to be

a branch of our own gas, a collection of clouds,
an extension of the Milky Way's dust.

In cosmic clarity, measurable variations,
brightness, then dimness—a literal star is born.

She releases light-years of fluted music to my ears,
an inalienable, distant distinction.

We are not alone.

1924

The Road Atlas Less Traveled

Two road atlases submerged in a glove box,
And sad I could not grasp both maps,
And be well-traveled, charted 'round global clock,
And stretch my wings like a broad-bound hawk
Over Great River Road and Cumberland Pass;

Then turn, adroitly, according to gravel guide,
And taking perhaps a by-way, betwixt
To graze my radials where nimblewill hides
And treat my Detroit treads to a scenic ride;
Petrified Forest, Cadillac Ranch along Route 66;

And with navigable notes, I, the self-able chauffer,
Pave my way, AAA, past bluebird diner, motel
Survey hard and soft surfaces like a first soldier,
Put weight of world's pavements on my Titan-tired shoulders,
And drive toward destiny, come highway heaven or hell.

I shall be pulling over to the breakdown lane, with a sigh—
My damn hand is stuck; odds of roadside assistance, slim
What with my fingers, right fist in mess of papers, entwined
Inside this cramped compartment like a wrathful grapevine—
Where is Rand McNally when you need him?

1925

H. L. Mencken Notes on Scopes Trial

We are a mere quarter in this 100-year charge,
And, yet, I have a distinct, gut inkling
These dates in Dayton will lead to the trial of our century.

A maze of apes sits like imbeciles on the court lawn
Dawning firm summer hats, set opinions
Before the first sworn testimony given.

Ah, God—
My God, your God, our creative, collective God—
That is what all this arrest and arrangement is about.

I doubt this biology guy, this infidel teacher Scopes has much chance.
The pool of buffoons serving on this July jury
Resemble nothing more than uninformed farmers, pat church-goers.

The *Holy Bible* should have a heyday, this week, in Tennessee.
Why, I am surprised its pressed scriptures are not being dispensed
In the outer hickory halls of tempered hysteria.

At least, the charming town has treated the attorneys well:
William Jennings Bryan prepared to fire away for the Prosecution—
Clarence Darrow biting at prime bit to impugn the Butler Act.

The simian issue of evolution is second instrument here
Among the pewed and stewed, bubbling just
Beneath boiling point to glorify God's holy word from gavel to gavel.

After opening remarks,
My primary concern in this primate witches' burn
Rests not with Scopes, for he won't win.

No, my sleeve of unease tugs for Bryan,
Hot from fervid-throat collar, sweat flinging from oratorical chin.
I'm afraid this Lord-fearing labyrinth will be the death of him.

1926

It's Not So Semple

Praise Jesus and the Lord Almighty!
Can your angelic ears hear me?
Won't your miraculous minds believe me?

Why, evangelicalism is as American
as a clean-up Yankee batter grand slam,
a slice or your grandmother's fruit-jar pie.

I am Aimee Semple McPherson, I am!
May all of your mortality and penance turn to ash.
But, before you exhale—and go, donate to my radio show.

Remit my megachurch,
you sin-clad lurch,
and when you pay, pay in cash.

All aboard! This ship of faithful fools!
You're the soul-touristed tool.
I'm the sainted palm, Psalms precursor—

to the likes
of Bakker, Falwell, and Swaggart, sir,
whose awful profits

turn from
heaven, then
turn to trash.

1927

Spirit of St. Louis

Surely, this flight must be easier
than delivering the mail
from St. Louis to Chicago
by air in winter.

It is not so much
the limited-vision periscope to my left side,
single-span wing, or safety net of extra fuel—
but this hour-angle watch
that serves as best mate, trans-Atlantic tool.

It's all in the cockpit wrist.

Both almanac and sextant,
its hands help to determine the monoplane's longitude.
(Latitude is easy.
You just scan an ocean of sky for the sun.)

With no parachute, radar, or radio set,
I cannot think of failure,
the fallen souls who flew before me—dead, injured, disappeared.

Fatigue, deprivation of sleep—
like the paired-continental course itself is non-stop.

I must keep my iced-over eyes on the Orteig Prize—
a tailspin of fame, further aerial exploration, a world's worth of merit.

Night descends.
I bend the fuselage-frame, downward,
toward initial flickers of land—
then a lantern-waving crowd at Le Bourget
guiding me to touchdown
with cylindered, city lights of Paris.

1928

Steamboat Willie

The animated short film
hit on all three whistles:

gag-and-speed visual effects,
wide distribution,
& synchronized sound.

Sound. Sound!
It must've been sheer sheet music
to Walt Disney's ears.

It's a sketchy business: riverboat work.

What with a top-tappin', foot-stompin' rodent
at temporary, whistlin'-wheel helm—
when there are smoke-stacked floors to soap,
livestock to cargo,
potatoes to peel,
mocking parrot to kill.

And a-shore, Steamboat Minnie needs a riparian lift.
Hook her by pliant bloomers.
Whisker her flower-pot hat on board.
Then, wind up "Turkey in the Straw"
from the ukulele-eating goat.

It's a portrait Georgia O'Keeffe forgot to paint.

All hands, transparently overlaid, on deck!
All limbs, rubber hose!

1929

Satchmo

Jazz will bring an end to things—
a blue evening, final smoke of a decade.

And this man Satchmo,
his solo riffs will set your mood—swinging—
in an off-beat,
                improvised sway.

If you want to catch his hectic sound,
I heard he took his horn and pipes
to the Big Apple
where "Pops" performs best
when he misbehaves.

He's the gravelly-throat toast and trumpet
of Hudson Theater's *Hot Chocolate* revue,
Upper Manhattan.

(Just blocks beneath his blares, Wall Street is about blow.)

But Louie will play on,
his syncopated star to peak,
                                        gigs later,
at Harmonia Gardens—
when he belts out to Dolly—

Hello!

1930

The Hays Code

If I formally rebuke the expurgator,
do I censure the censor?

Why can't I watch Norma Shearer
slip out of an even sheerer slip?

Damn! I mean, *golly-gee-gadzooks,*
the Motion Picture Producers and Distributors of America!

No lewd nudity, indelicate delicates—

Put britches on the lubricious.

Nix the dark-and-gnarly in licentious betwixt.

Roll thick wool or tweed around all things obscene.
Put a fastidious lid on prurient undressin'.

This quest for decency
                                        puts moral turpitude on perturbed run.

Why should the flappin' 20s have all the fun?

I think I'll flop down on my heat-resistant couch

in a Great Depression.

1931

Empire State Building

With everything these days—
down
stocks, employment, morale—

it rises in New York horizon
like a stone testament of triumph,
Art Deco bastion-blade
scraping civic sky.

Even the greyhound nimbuses
hovering its spire
unleash and glisten in sleek efficiency.

Surely, this is spring, a grand opening.
Business lifts from dirt and grit—
and blooms.

And stories, so many stories to climb and tell.

There, on Fifth Avenue base,
enters an engaging man,
a dandy with a clutch of spined roses.
He is hopeful as a firm handshake.
Upon an elevated, panoramic floor,
his enterprising intent is to give
a special client
a ring.

Ah! This steel scale will make heaven's headlines.

Then, the world's tallest building will be even bigger box office—
when its cinder-slab tiles
receive an unexpected tenant and toothy smile
from Skull Island.

1932

Hooverville

Not exactly a nightingale singing in Berkeley Square, is it?
The ash and ache photograph of a Hooverville near a reservoir
deep in the bleed of Central Park.
And don't forget the shantytowns erected along Highway 66
from Mississippi to Bakersfield—
strewn like bits of Wall Street ticker-tape waste,
Hoover blankets, Hoover Pullmans—
his name a Proper Adjective for anything ruinous, bad, *depressed* —
1929 prohibitive, hung over, unemployed,
its undernourished body distended into the 1930s.
Boy, I can see him now, through rose-colored—no—
make that Depression glass.
Young Herbert, Bertie, growing up among prairie grasses, modest cottages—
between Main and Downey, son of a blacksmith, mowing the mayor's lawn,
hanging a horseshoe like a yuletide wreath over a widow's back door,
son of a Quaker, orphaned by age ten, to Oregon.
He is a manhood away from his engineer mastery,
a dozen love letters from the one Stanford-stamped to Lou,
several appointments away from Oval environs, a nation's mood swing away
from being despised and adored.

Hoover called the Great Depression a *transitory paralysis,*
but them's fightin' words to farmers throwing milk and fits
onto Devil's Highway, bread line queued to next county.
So, America engineered a few false attributes,
built a great wall, to the truth about Hoover—
Hoover the Diplomat rescued Chinese children,
during Dragon rounds, Boxer Rebellion.
We *au revoired* the fact Hoover the Humanitarian saved, brought home
thousands of tourists from beleaguered France.
Our tastes waffled at the idea:
Hoover the Keeper of Good Commerce fed the entire country of Belgium—
when Brussels was overrun by the Germans, had no francs in its pants.

Hooverville

Hooverville

Even environmentalists casted doubts about Hoover the Conservationist—
but he cared, indeed, about our ecology—down to the last salmon.
During post-WW-II reconstruction, Democrat Truman didn't give him hell;
he gave Republican Hoover a top job.
Scapegoat, scholar, rumored to be British,
Hoover knew the presidency was a shrewd, elusive bird,
so, he took no seed-pence for it. Not exactly a nightingale—whistling away—
but a hard-luck meadowlark caught in a spare-a-dime cage.
Indeed, they were hard times, but, America, you'd be hard pressed
to find another like the West Branch wonder, first in flight 'to the West Wing'
who, when he vacated a table of many hats, left a room of empty seats.

1933

Ramping Up the Presidency

Inconspicuous as possible,
two new ramps, coded as "Dayton articles," were built
south side of stately White House
near the West Wing and Residence back entrances,
to accommodate the incoming,
landslide-winning president,
clandestine construction,
surreptitious slopes,
supervised by the Secret Service,
who also used codes for mobility aids,
such as canes, crutches, braces.

Disability was to be privately embraced,
a personal platform issue, not for public show.

FYI, FDR designed many of his wheelchairs himself,
narrow kitchen-throne creations for easy passage
through executive-branch corridors,
that enabled the Chief to get
from point A   to point B.

The country rarely caught a scant eye
of the 32nd president, entering or exiting—
a doorway, a foyer, a hall.
He preferred to be seated to greet his fellow citizens—
settled for a fireside chat with the American people
to prate upon the matters of a day:
the Bank Crisis, New Deal, Currency Situation.

The nation was all ears, leaning in
for the next spark-idea for recovery.

And, if one strategy wouldn't serve,
President Roosevelt wheeled on—
in circular works of his mind—going from Plan A to Plan B.

1934

Dillinger & Dust

Together, they are rivals to the title:
Public Enemy No. 1.

Each, a black blizzard,
exploiting a bountiful drought of opportunity
whittling away at precious forces,
natural resources of Great Plains
like a signature, break-out thief
carving a wooden gun—

both armed bullies
stealing top dollar and topsoil
from trusted safes and landscapes
of Middle America—

pointlessly pursued
by cops and conservationists,

rising in notoriety
to a formidable wall of fear
and wind-shaken headlines—

a set of saboteurs to systems—
birth brothers to the Dirty Thirties—

gangster & grit

heartless partners
in crime.

1935

Murals of the New Deal Era

Many of them hang like stretched, picturesque stamps
along post-office walls,
commissioned and funded in the 30s & 40s
by the US Treasury,
(not so much FDRs Works Progress Administration)
to depict the lavish landscapes of America,
the country's muscle
upon permanent surfaces
that offset transient terrors,
momentous miseries of the Great Depression.

Sculpted in glazed tempera
(that's right, folks, egg yolks)
to cast vibrant representations, in dust-free colors,
of the farmers, industrialists, settlers, domestics
who plant, plow, and produce
with flexed arms, enveloped in denim
beneath bustling smokestack, or bountiful farm—

these flat, free-to-see masterpieces—each—
create a fixed exhibit
born from a brush's steadfast quiver.

There is proof in hold-tight paint,
during turbulent, threadbare times
our government still had a few gems in the bag—
and, best of all—
could still deliver.

1936

Rose of Sharon

after The Grapes of Wrath, novel by John Steinbeck

All dust-drive long,
I minded and coddled
my unborn child
with wishful ideas, self-pity,
and preoccupied prayer.

I was all pick-of-the-peach dreams,
tending to California comfort,
mother-in-waiting, secretive things
about to be brought forth from such fertile valleys
of that fruited state—
and furrowed within me.

The grapes hung in the West
from a shooted vine of Divine distance—I trusted.

Nothing, no weeded corruption
banked upon our tumble wheels
stalled my troth in immaculate fruition.

Now, upon golden arrival,
I fall, an abandoned ma'am crying
over maternal milk unspilled, unused—baby-barren,
my drunkard husband,
high-tailed like a runaway deer—
leaving a family of one.

In this whispering barn,
it is as if winds of the red country,
gray country have trailed me here,
mocking my ignorance, giving last tufts of air
to suffocating delusion.

Rose of Sharon

Rose of Sharon

All that remains is my bloated bosom,
deflated cradle of a crushed goddess' urn—
and a rib-reckoned, stranger-man—yonder
suckling starvation in the crook of a corner.

I hoist my ample, robbed body—
walk a field of faith toward him,
offer my cistern of loosened breasts
to parched crack of his lips.

We are pacified in bruised exchange of *hush-now* concern.

1937

Dwarfed

The final rivet drilled
at Golden Gate Bridge,
its ceremonial guild
could not outshine
a peripatetic septet of small pines
walking, whistling *heigh-ho*, a-toe,
in a faraway forest.

The Hindenburg
exploding overhead,
its flames of Hellish hydrogen
could not outspread
the magic mirror's word-to-the-wicked
of a fairer face
who bit grave dust—and apple red.

A vast overpass
at Frisco Bay—overshadowed,
a disastrous dirigible—
lain to ashes upon Jersey meadow,
one does not need a Doctorate to see how Dopey, Bashful,
and compressed company—
leave a larger, trailblazing impression—nothing short, of extraordinary.

1938

Thornton Wilder's *Our Town*

I say the Stage Manager is God—
omniscient, omnipotent—
manipulating time warps and fine folks
of Grover's Corners, New Hampshire,
like a pensive puppeteer,
delivering wise, reflective lines
routinely—throughout the course
of sparsely-scenic, three-act play—
just as Howie Newsome or that Crowell kid
deliver bottled milk or morning newspaper.

In his mundane monologues, matter-of-fact narration,
that Otherworldly Auteur reminds us:

The sun rises, and we rise with it.

Then, like invincible, cyclical clockwork,
we move to an invisible master—work, school, garden snap peas, repeat.

We've only the time to tell loved ones—
we haven't the time.

There is always the next inevitable thing.
And we gotta run; we gotta go.

Babies are born. Daughters married. Mothers laid in premature graves.
And through it all,
the Stage Manager interjects, interrupts, intravenously feeds
an anemic, awestruck audience
how extraordinary the ordinary is—yes, it's wonderful and horrible
and fleeting like the 5:45 a.m. train whistling its distant roll.

And amidst this mobile madness,
that Divine Director claims something, inside, is eternal—a shared universal.
I say it's the soul.

1939

Oz with the Wind

It was a good year for color in film:
yellow bricks, ruby shoes, an emerald city,
and Scarlet O'Hara.
Technicolor™ in trademark—
a blue yearning for Kansas home-place,
a Sherman orange burning of plantation estates,
a silver woodsman clad in empty tin,
a cowardly cat dragged in pink ribbons.

And there is something recurrent
about all this wind—how it takes a denim-bibbed girl
from pig-pen here to witch's spin there—
how it sweeps a divided-dirt country
to doormat of despair.

And a very good year—
for men in shifty shades of support—
ex-beaus who don't give a damn,
a brainless scarecrow
who helps a runaway niece
in a foreign jam.

And, lastly, a great year
to learn
summoned monkeys can fly,
green curtains can convert
to a dress in a bind,
that water will cause
the wicked to vanish—
and a spoiled girl
somewhere over the smoke of Savannah—
yes, she can survive,
by clutching to tomorrow's dreams
and a radish.

1940

What's Shaking in San Bernadino?

This is a super-seismic flip, not about earthquakes,
but two brothers with a couple of spatulas—and a faultless dream—
that will, nevertheless, split into franchises, frustration, and fortune—
that will end on the salty side of Drive-Thru Social Darwinism.

But for now,
before hot dog-eats-hot dog,
it is customer enjoys burger—a fast, flavorful burger,
on this California desert day in May.
Yes, two hamburger-huckster brothers,
Richard and Maurice McDonald, "Dick" and "Mac,"
both well content flipping patties for quick profit, non-stop,
like a pair of small-business pops.

And it is all about speed, a minimalist menu—and more speed—
a streamlined, well-prepped assembly ready to slab the cheese,
squirt fresh ketchup, mustard—sprinkle onion, deftly place two tart pickles—
then wrap and warm under a heating lamp.

Friendly carhops serve you with a sandwich, fries, and drink—with a wink.

The outdoor seating counter occupied from opening line to sunset.
Hungry, habitual teens have their hangout amidst whisps of sand—
loyal customers steady as a valley breeze.

Money rolls in like tumbleweeds with spirited tow.

Thar's gold in them thar foothills!

I know, my trusted brother. How far do you think this bun-bliss will go?

I don't know, Dick. But we need more milkshake mixers.

You got it, Mac. I'll call up that salesman from Chicago.

1941

Pearl Harbor

I'd hate to be the pearl
harboring inside that Oahu oyster shell.
The only neck I'd be wrapped around—
would be my sunken own.

What purpose is a harbor, anyway?
To protect ships from storms at sea—Hmmm.

And it seems the United States of America
cannot criticize itself without complimenting itself, first.

The Sleeping Giant—
the bombing of Pearl Harbor, the sacking of sailors, US Pacific Fleet,
at least, woke the Dormant Mountain to Hitler's
egregious encroachments in Europe,
the Nazi Party's perilous propaganda flying about
oceanic theaters of the world.

Ah, Infamy!
Now, there's a word that survives a Sunday morning pummeling,
stands above Hell and Sabbath's smoked water, alone. *Infamy.*

A petrol sky subsumes dawn's bridal white.

I wonder—
does anyone waking, today, in the conterminous, contiguous 48 states—
speak Japanese, or Hawaiian?

If so,
Bakudan, Koloa maoli—

They have bombs in Japan, you know—ship/
splitting ones.
They have ducks in Hawaii, you know—
sitting ones.

1942

A Riveting War Effort

The poster of Rosie the Riveter
flexing "*We Can Do It*" muscle
won't win this war by bicep alone.

She, too, will need a gun—
a rivet gun, or pneumatic hammer,
to drive the steel force
that fastens two metal pieces, and our country, together.

And Uncle Sam—
he needs your empty toothpaste-tube tin
for food-can rations to soldiers,
airplane instrument panels,
ammo boxes, and containers for medical supplies
like blood plasma and morphine syringes.

Every bit counts.

War is a hungry machine—
insatiable with its corporal cravings,
five-star commands for military morsels
to provide home-front, factory cooking
to serve, course-by-course, its appetite for arms, overseas.

Head, shank, and tail—everybody does its part.

Bandana Betty, doff your apron. Ignite that weld.
Even the local toy train company converts its tracks to shells.

Our troops don't need cars; they bleed for tanks.

The War Protection Board gives its orders—

and obliging thanks.

1943

Norman Rockwell's Four Freedoms

1 FREEDOM OF SPEECH

From stuffed town hall meeting,
a flannel man rises from citizen twine
to allot a string of thought,
to speak his yarn of mind.

2 FREEDOM OF WORSHIP

Everyday disciples from diverse range
of denomination, sect—gather in conscience collect—
profiles of prayer, a tacit silhouette of suggestion—
people free to believe, at liberty to question.

3 FREEDOM FROM WANT

Atop plates a-plenty, we close-knit kin
lean toward feast of bird, with pert chins, wide-eyed,
then lower grateful heads for bounty and bread
upon graced table of Grandma's and Lord's provide.

4 FREEDOM FROM FEAR

My children, your cozy minds of peace, entrenched
inside warm sheets when charge of darkness comes,
for sleep is for eased heart's safe-keeping
and phantoms of dancing sugar plums.

1944

Anne Frank of the Attic

This is not the release I wanted,
a kind of sinister, simmering endurance
where the brush of a kitten
or tap of a porcelain cup
summons instant seizure,
eventual death.

I can change letters, sentences,
thoughts, whole pages,
but I cannot transform the war.

My mother is near me,
but I am far from her arms.

My family and the huddled others
live as a sort of one-celled creature,
unified fear, programmed effect,
confined to the cause of the Party.

We lie about the attic like trunks of old clothes.

I come here, not to veiled annex,
but to you, Diary, for refuge and sanctuary,
your bindings attuned,
open to original hope.

As routine as the hours are practiced and pass,
the atmosphere breaks each daylight, in silence,
to a disheartening divide.

Beyond the bookshelf downstairs,
there is a hissing.

I surmise it is either a tea kettle or spy.

1945

Enola Gay

Named for the pilot's mother,
I course my way
through expectant weather—
gravid, full of firestorm, charring history,
with a compelling child,
Little Boy,
inside my bomb-bay womb.

This is the mum of all deliveries.

Quiet, maternal instinct tells me:
This kid will be a kicker,
quite a riotous gunner,
the splitting image of his physicist father—
once his nuclear head is released
from my fuselage frame.

Induced by an altitude near heaven,
I come to term with birth of destruction.

An August sky—
pristine and cloudless

a perfect day for black rain.

1946

Churchill Unveils the Iron Curtain in Missouri

I would've guessed Winston's famous speech
to be set somewhere in London proper,
the Palace of Westminster, for instance,
or at marbled footsteps of a cathedral
named for a patron saint.

What in the Show-Me sakes is he doing in Missouri?
President Truman, no doubt, brought the British Bulldog here.
At least, this speaking venue in Fulton is Westminster College,
an acoustic semblance perhaps to home.

My, this gent can turn a phrase,
claiming America is at its "pinnacle of power,"
calling for shields against "two giant marauders—
war and tyranny."

His fervent tone makes me want to strap on double-buckle combat boots
and safeguard an innocent village, overseas.

The former prime minister's word grouping of "sinews of peace"
resonates with devoted crowd.
It suggests strength and calm are a responsibility
of the United States and United Kingdom.
His oration becomes saturated with "we."
A "special relationship" to form a United Nations Organization,
prepared and fortified to defend the free world.

The celebratory ticker-tape has yet to be swept off Broadway,
its Canyon of Heroes honoring the homecoming from World War II.

To conclude, the high minister speaks of a shadow fallen over Soviet Russia,
an "Iron Curtain," behind which Eastern Europe bonds, a communal hold.

The image sticks to each attendant ear like blood on a wall.
After a warm reception, the mid-century's air turns cold.

1947

Cheers to You, Mr. Robinson

Your signature debut,
it will integrate, put a dotted-line end
to dugout custom, same-skin tradition,
the expected star-spangled white line-up
of baseball season.

Oh, you'll still know Jim Crow, beanballs, strikes—
from biased umpires, and insecure types—
(who threaten to throw another kind of strike)—
from organized players seeing color-line red
at your "Jersey-42" plate and base discipline,
hefty collection of stolen bases,
sell-out crowds at Ebbets, Doubleday, Wrigley Fields—
Yankee Stadium, and Polo Grounds.

And to barrier-bound, racist rivals
who'd rather see your Dodger blue a-blaze
in the Devil's warm-up deck, below—

their children's children's children
will see your legacy on radiant display
at Cooperstown.

1948

Dewey Defeats Truman

An egg-on-face sonnet

With a brood of newspapers
across free-range nation
giving Dewey's grit candidacy
editorial support, upper leg—
a cocky Windy City column
that tapped the New York governor
broke out white-foaming kegs;
but when, at a trilling St. Louis train stop,
a win-feathered, laurel-teethed Truman
clutched in triumphant hands
the *Tribune's* erroneous crow, headline dispatch,
it became broth-clear the disgraced *Daily*
counted its pick-'em chickens
before electoral eggs had hatched.

1949

First Snowfall in Los Angeles

Meticulous weather fanatics
may dig and sway
to differ,
by my Midwest mentality prefers
to mull over
the accumulative bing
of white-stuff
that beclouded orange groves,
swept and stuck
in Bernadino streets, outskirt canyons
of *film-noir* L. A.,

as first drift in Hollywood,

causing the green-palmed Southland
those shaded, blue gardenia-ed Californians
to throw fits and snowballs
at occluded traffic, polar irony—
anything within wind-up, boulevard range—
as if climate-stiffened citizens,
those pampered screen-testers were primed
to accept inevitability
of coming extremities, arrhythmic change
in fine lines of powder—
reminiscent of last night's binge
of hush producer's
party cocaine.

1950

McCarthyism

Subversive is such a powerful, catalytic word—
a descriptive dirge, rather,
hideous sound from the Underground, undermining—
putting to rest—innocent souls.

It raises suspicion and lowers stern brow.

Place the slinky adjective, *McCarthythist,*
in front of noun generalities
like e*lement, personnel,* or *behavior,*
and an entire Wheeling, West Virginia, hotel auditorium
whispers and worries—
Which witch hunt is which?—
the long country ride, take-me-home.

But, say, you hold a *list,* Senator, in your hand,
dangle your tyrannical tab
in front of a women's political club like slab-doctrine,
yes, a dark list, black becoming, of known enemies
who are seated within our government offices,
perched beneath tax-dollar desks
with treasonous knees—

Well, that's a horse of a different dolor-color.

Your finger-file makes oratorical fright—concrete,
fills those lunch-lady hats
with feathers of dread—
seals the paranoid State Department deal—
gives birth to patriotic persecution—
gets the Communist Party departed—
triggers a fist-pumping vessel
to see and scare Red.

1951

I Love Lucy, Too

She had me at nightclub.
As in, *Ricky, I want to star in your nightclub.*
    Ethel, let's take a cab to see what Ricky is doing at the nightclub.
    Fred Mertz, why isn't my husband at the nightclub?

(I always suspected the Tropicana troubadour was cheating on
his stir-crazy, red-head housewife, even in syndication.
He just seemed too darn content with those twin beds   apart.
That, and when Ricardo ambled through charming apartment door,
at all hours, the man's ruffled pantalones looked like his act had already
lit and smoked that fat Cuban cigar.)

But this is not about suspected infidelity
drummed with some feathered filly
from a Manhattan conga show—it's not.

This is about infectious sitcom laughter
from generations of audiences
who seek no cure,
no network contract termination
of a zany bellwether
stomping grapes and picking local-color fights in Italian vineyard,
stuffing assembly-line, quasi-wrapped chocolates in factory hat,
guzzling rerun spoonsful of *Vitameatavegamin* until daffy-drunk.

Funny, Mrs. Ricardo, funny.

My hiccup heart
only wishes it had met you
when you were Miss McGillicuddy.

1952

The Cold War Mushrooms

Mushroom is one
of those multi-operative words.
It can serve as noun or verb,
depending on context,
like ring, or water, or book.

War is often about language, phrasing:
Atomic Age, Cold War, Operation Ivy.

Why, give a mission
of terrible fission-fusion testing
a catchy moniker, federal funding, tropical location—
and the post-war arms race is on.

I just might give Senator Stevenson a *ring.*
Ask him to *water* down those pesky nuclear trials
to save a pod of dolphins, an archipelago of islanders.
So, my family and I can *book* a vacation
on a Pacific atoll, surrounded by nothing
but coral and calm—

before more versatile terms mushroom,
burden our world—like—
We bomb to keep peace
or
peacekeeping hydrogen bomb.

1953

The Execution of Julius and Ethel Rosenberg

Prison lords of Sing Sing shepherd Ethel through its catacombs.

Purse-lipped, tight-eyed, she is stoic as cryptic tomb that awaits her.

Her husband, Julius, dwells elsewhere in a firing chair,
waiting electrocution.

In charred back-to-back succession, they die, just before sundown—
of Jewish Sabbath night,
for alleged transmission of atomic sketches to Soviets.

Frail Julius slouches, limp, at jolt of three.
Reticent Ethel requires five volts,
then droops before a table of her enemies.

Across choppy Hudson River,
inside a New Jersey Cold War orphan home,
their boys, Michael and Robert,
comfort one another in goodness and mercy.

1954

Walking Through Town with Linda Brown

Winters in Topeka are the worst—
no hills or tall structures to block
cold, harsh winds blowing from wide Kansas plain.

I cry walking the required miles to school, Monroe Elementary,
on horrible mornings like these.

Tears freeze on my cheeks, breaking the skin—
brown skin, black skin—
which means I must continue to plod on—
past the white limestones walls
of Sumner School
where I am banned like an outlaw to attend—
Sumner School, near my home,
Sumner—with its warm hallways carved
in a privileged wood.
Sumner, which looks so much like *Summer,*
when freezing rain and sleet
obscure my path, true vision.

My soaked shoes make snow tracks between divided train tracks
of a railroad switchyard.
I come across a hectic, ice-rink avenue,
busy as ever with bustling cars.
I dodge their steel fenders with scurrying, third-grade feet.

At last,
I trudge to the bus stop for black girls and boys—
a stigma on wheels
to take our separate selves to a distant school.

I step aboard—iron out my weathered taupe coat—
pained, but proud—ready to go, ready to learn—
ready to join the vehicle's igniting
fury and fuel.

1955

The Back Seat

Who wants to take the subordinate back seat?

Who wants to ride second fiddle to trumpeted strings of bigotry?

Who wants to plant dowdy derrière on such an inferior chair?

Who wants to lower downtrodden soul upon an even lower totem pole?

What wants to be focus-fuss on such a demeaning transit bus?

Who wants to park a rosy bum behind a white line reserved for paler ones?

Not me. Not you.

My butt and thighs have better things to do
like stride for civil rights,
or assume position for Salk's polio vaccine.

1956

The Pelvis of Elvis

Screw his blue swede shoes.
It was his pelvis that made Elvis, *Elvis.*
What most people needed to support their gait—
The King of Rock 'n Roll shook and shimmered
to conquer *The Milton Berle Show* and screaming-teen world.

Throwin' craps, crackin' the whip, toe-tippin'
The Memphis Flash proved
that new, ungodly music—
was all in his heavenly hips.

Ah! The pelvis, digestion's great protector.
The pelvis. Did you know it has a floor?
The pelvis.
Who knew something so sacrum
could be controversial and adored?

But, in that Graceland bathroom, decades later—
one hot August afternoon,
did his pelvis forsake him?

Did it thrust to a bust
as Ol' Snake Hips bumped, grunted, and grinded
to go number one
or two?

You'd think a timeless icon
who could move married mamas
to toss their seamless panties on a stage—
could make his own bowels
seamlessly move.

1957

I (Still) Like Ike

Pin the bouncing button on me, again.
It's been four *cold* years,
but I still like Ike.

Nuclear tests are like elephant drums to my ears.
The folks tuck and fret in a fallout shelter,
but I still like Ike.

"More bang for the buck" has free world in a welter.
Diplomacy creeps to missile-bow brink,
but I still like Ike.

Best minds of Congress obsessed with what Communists think.
Paranoia runs an interstate's course,
but I still like Ike.

I still like Ike! I still like Ike!
And when I turn twenty-one,
I'll vote for a candidate just like him. (I might.)

1958

The Fad-u-lous Fifties

We'll bop in our socks
'til *Hound Dog* rocks around a Comet's clock.

Our hand-jivin' hips twist with rugged beatniks, that poetry set,
clad in black—why, we might even *coffeehouse* experiment.

The Hula-Hoop's™ a whoop; James Dean's a drive-in draw.
Are you happy to see me in 3-D, or are you sportin' a conical bra?

The soda fountain may be nothing new,
but it's got a chrome jukebox and an egg cream, jerked for two.

Let's mold our nifty love in gelatin—which flavor is flirt?
Me in my coonskin cap, you in your poodle skirt.

1959

Achoo & Aloha

ALASKA

Statehood is nothing to sneeze at;
yet how fitting,
in spruce of winter,
frozen feds have chosen
this glacial gem
to join contiguous forty-eight
beneath its
Last Frontier rim.

I heard the ptarmigan will be state bird—
a nice, iced selection, arctic apropos—
if only jaded photographers can find
the spotless partridge
camouflaged in blotless tufts
of snow.

HAWAII

Statehood is something to erupt about;
yes, how spitting,
in juice of summer,
legislative leis have ordained
this lava-surfing gem
to join the forty-eight—ashore
beyond its
subtropical stem.

I heard the nēnē will be state bird—
a goosed choosing, short-winged swell,
if only its unique, low-to-high-pitched calls
could distinguish between
aloha and its rise, then fall
of hello and farewell.

1960

Hitting the Showers with Alfred Hitchcock

Embezzlement is draining.

To abscond with a windfall deposit
from your place of employment,
an insurance boss who trusts his loyal secretary—
why, it deluges the miscreant mind
with a jet stream of guilt,
tears at your conscience like frayed curtains,
flows through villainous veins
until you're unable to see the road   before you.

Soon, you're fragments of your former self.

Marion Crane feels dirty, not skin dirty,
but soul dirty, a soiled spirit, in need of a come-cleaning.
$40,000 wrapped in butcher paper like a leg of lamb,
the star-crossed adulteress is on the lam—
driving herself and her '57 Ford, California-crazy—
until the impulsive perp pulls over for a peaceful night's rest
at Bates Motel.

The proprietor, Norman Bates, is kind, soft-spoken, even charming—
but his mind is a fly-infested swamp.

Uphill at the house,
Mother disapproves of such a voluptuous guest,
frets her beloved boy might be looking for a wet wife.

Poor Norman himself is a split drape, torn
between that graying, slash-mouth shrew—off her rocker—
and the disrobing Psyche from Phoenix in first rental room.

No, inhospitable Mother Bates refuses to share
even a plate of sandwiches with Miss Crane at late supper,
but at nozzle time, she will dish out—a knife.

1961

Marvel™ Us

I confess.
I am not a comic-book aficionado.
And when I first caught wind of The Fantastic Four™,
I thought the obscure quartet was a collective set— stripped or—
spawned from a spider, bat, kryptonite, and big-breasted Amazon.

Wrong.

I also believed DC™ meant those series were published
from our nation's capital. Wrong. Wrong.

If there is something I got correct from years of comic cluelessness,
it is, perhaps, this:

Space scientists
Reed Richards™, Sue Storm-Richards™, Johnny Storm™, and Ben Grimm™—
formed the first widespread, widely-read, recurring dysfunctional family
in American pop culture history.

All thanks to cosmic rays.

That's right. That's it. Sun spit…hit those four void-explorers
creating Mr. Fantastic™, Invisible Woman™ Human Torch™, and Thing™.

And I further confess.
I am not well- versed enough to detail or describe the Multiverse™, or any
alternate universe or alternative universe that this alternative force
may have penetrated, populated, or saved.

All I know is—somewhere along the superhero line—
Mr. Fantastic™ married Invisible Woman™, who is Human Torch's™ sister,
which means Human Torch™ is the brother-in-law to Mr. Fantastic™.
Thing™ must be quarried in there somehow. What a s-t-r-e-t-c-h!
I have trademarked™ this poem to death.
(Maybe Elixir™ can revive it.)

1962

Year on the Brink

The word *brink* has an unnerving,
unwelcoming connotation about it.
It suggests, to some,
that a precipice, an edge—
is about to reach its summit-limit.
Something is about to fall—
be it political patience
or prices—
and the engrossed world—
paused—in anticipation of inevitable tailspin—
it will never be the same.

In Cuba,
the brink bearers are Soviet missiles,
Castro's host of thermonuclear catapults
delivered from Khrushchev's Kremlin—
bay-stationed and posed
toward a leaf-shaking America
in endless October.

In Rogers, Arkansas,
the brink courier is Walmart™,
Sam Walton's boast of customer-is-king retail stores
discounted from a low-charging business model
steeped and situated
toward a finite set of grief-quaking
five-and-dime, Mom-and-Pop shops.

1963

For Whom the Grass Knolls

With bluebonnet flowers,
a lone-star lot of foothill children
make-believe braid
a love field of their nob own—
skipping little-star looks
and primary school books
for a freaky Friday
with JFK.

They gather in grass with black nannies,
shake a stick of better-colored banners.

The sky tolls a cloud of deposits.
Book it Marine blue.

Raised on Belt beliefs,
oil's concrete,
the curbside kids sit
their citified breeches
down for a morning tyke-scare
on Dallas' Elm Street.

A fallen November
leaf and a Motorcade
turns. First bullets,
then bulletins break a nation's heart
with grave, groundbreaking news.

The high-heeled luncheon at the Dallas Trade Mart
not so much canceled—
but first course is chauffeured in, untouched, grim.

For Whom the Grass Knolls

A congress of beehives and flipped bobs
pray among swan-scarved napkins,
atop estate-a-plate tables
for an autumnal-themed, attendant God
to fall-weather it all, yonder—within.

Back at the blood drive,
Texas toddlers stain their pink cheeks
with why-me rain,
wobble their wat'nit, pained knees
with witness green.

Up, up from staid gray,
a force-one plane flies away—
sowing its wild oaths—
all awash to Washington—
with a pillbox-tiered princess and tearless LBJ,
like an airborne, convertible presidency
democracy's done-away dream—
Camelot gone, shady, gone—
in a runaway, brainless limousine.

1964

Ladies and Gentlemen, The Beatles!

They are the type of invasion
American youth have been longing for—
mop-headed musicians
manned with pop-hit ammunition.

The Fab Four—
Paul, John, George & Ringo—
stage a rock-n-roll raid
on *The Ed Sullivan Show.*

Clad in dark Chesterfield jackets,
toting an army of electric guitars,
The Beatles give defenseless teens, shrieking girls
the loony swoons.

With a record Nielsen rating of 45.3,
the coiffed quartet hold hands with half a nation—
not bloody bad for a quaternity
of lyrical lieutenants from Liverpool.

1965

Folk Music on a Rock 'n' Roll

Unlike a rolling stone,
a gem of a hit record gathers moss—
fans, groupies, maniacs, enthusiasts, a list of critics, aficionados.

And what better way
to scale a pop chart
than to laugh at, disdain, encourage, lament
a once-upon-a-time socialite
who has fallen off her high mount?

Dylan called the original draft
of his cranked-organ classic, *vomit*,
or maybe he was confusing
President Johnson's draft revisions
with his own Woodstock-rock infusion.

And what to make of his tambourine's target—
Miss Lonely?

The downtrodden damsel is out there—
spin-after-spin,
peddling bleak street,
in a sidewalk sea of anonymity,
trying to avoid the Highway's hapless cracks
of Expectation's poverty,
waging her own wageless war
against an oath-spoken Great Society.

Like a Brooklyn wind that's blowing—
at least, she's free.

1966

Bellwether

I wonder
if the carillon bells
from the Texas Tower rang on schedule,
each quarter-hour,
that fair-weather August morning, afternoon in Austin
when Charles Whitman bulleted his way
to headline fame as America's first—in a longhorn line— of mass shooters.

Forerunner of firearms,
trailblazer to decades of terror—
disguised as a custodian delivering repair equipment on a dolly of death,
he had time to arrange all seven weapons of choice
like spitting ducks in a row on the observation deck.

(Whitman told one hardware-store clerk
who sold him a couple of kid killers
that he was going *wild hog hunting* in Florida.)

96 minutes of shooting gallery practice on UT campus,
unlicensed artillery, magazine loads of victims,
pecan-sized, untreated tumor pressing
against the amygdala of his brain—
the madman in high-noon clock tower gunned down co-eds
like clay pigeons on the midway at state fair in Dallas,
with the wounded playing possum,
the mobile stooped behind trees, under decks, in dark stairwells.

Finally, a police officer named Houston fired lethal shots
at the ex-Marine's white headband.

It started to seep a hallelujah-red, leaving a permanent bloodstain.

Meanwhile,
The Eyes of Texas rang out from the Tower bells—all the live long day.

1967

Flowers in Your Hair, Football on the Field

Come together in California for the weekend.

I SAN FRANCISCO'S "HUMAN BE-IN"

Saturday, January 14th

At the height of tree-hugging Hippie Movement,
in psychedelic buses, dilapidated vans, packed Volkswagens™
the long-haired free spirits and bohemians, come.
Wreathed in dandelions, daisies, and peace signs—
they flock like denim-winged doves
to vast polo fields of Golden Gate State Park
to sit in, drop out—protest an unjust, imperialist war
that drags on their lips like a Bogart cigarette.
They gather to look for white rabbits in strawberry fields—
to merge a festival-feast of counterculture tribes
into one.
They come to lynch a long winter of hate,
to launch a "Summer of Love."

II THE FIRST SUPER BOWL™ 101

Sunday, January 15th

It was not a sellout.
And if you happened to be driving by the Coliseum in LA
on the 3900 block of South Figueroa Street
at 3 pm that day—
with $12 in your pocket—
well, mister, you could walk right in.
And it wasn't "Super" yet.
That rechristening media-darling moniker
would be the brainchild of Kansas City Chief's owner, Lamar Hunt.

Flowers in Your Hair, Football on the Field

The pigskin fanfare had some cumbersome title:
"The AFL-NFL World Championship Game,"
though the rest of the globe scarcely knew or played such sport.
And "Lombardi" wasn't a trophy yet,
he was a disciplined, convincing coach
of eventual winners—the Green Bay Packers.
The star of the game was quarterback Bart Starr.
(That homophone came in handy and catchy.)
And the star-studded half-time show was stages away—
from Janet's Jackson open-breasted display.
Instead, collegiate marching bands from Grambling, the U. of Arizona,
and a few high-steppers from Anaheim High
formed an outline of the United States
to the trumpeting sounds of Al Hirt
with the release of innumerable pigeons, balloons,
and a couple of jet-packed rocketeers.
CBS and NBC, both networks, carried the choreographed game.
The second-half kickoff had to be rebooted
when the Peacock's cameramen failed to follow the ball.
But there were commercials—
Goodyear™ claiming to be a "tire within a tire."
McDonald's™ boasting to be "the closest thing" to home cooking.
And TANG™ getting its orange groove on the spoon.
These 30-second spots cost thousands, not millions.
The Packers won. The Chiefs lost.
Each league brought its own sized footballs, network, and referees.
And, somewhere in all of this inaugural mix—
a troop of flag-bearing women dressed as George Washington,
suited in colonial garb to symbolize what the Super Bowl™ was meant to be:

revolutionary.

1968

Motel, Hotel Rooms to Rent

Rent as in shattered.

Rent as in torn.

Rent as in split apart—

a face, a nation

lying paralyzed, prostrate

on the Lorraine Motel

blood-stained, balcony floor.

Rent as in pieces.

Rent as in force.

Rent as in one country, asunder—

with no one

but an Ambassador Hotel busboy

to soothe a dying senator

along the back-kitchen corridor.

1969

Moon Riveting

It makes no imprint on me
which of these three
thick-suited space musketeers—
Armstrong, Aldrin, or Collins—
is first to walk on the moon.

I am guaranteed a firm foothold in history,
whichever of the silicon-soled boots
plants powder-traction on Sea of Tranquility.
I'll be there
like a Jackson 5 hit single.

What's his name is out.
You know, the astronaut born in Italy
who has to stay behind on command module *Columbia*
to orbit, alone, for hours
while Neil and Buzz have all the new frontier fun and newly found fame,
once the lunar module *Eagle* has landed.
You know, the guy's whose name sounds like a cocktail:
(*snap, snap, snap*) Michael Collins.

My best, balanced guess is that it will be Neil Armstrong
to be first gait out of the gate.
He's the big cheese on this floating satellite-sandwich.
It's probably an executive decision from NASA.
That, and the cabin's hatch opens sideways to provide him free range.

Still, the obstructed Aldrin is bound to make a thing of this.
He's military, with a doctorate in the vast blue field. Neil is civilian.

They can flip a crescent-shaped coin, for all I care.
I don't give a moon hydrangea's creep.
I, the invisible glue, on any foot to shoe.
I, one small step, will be first—
even before one giant leap.

1970

13 Seconds in Ohio

Spring carries no weapons,
unless you count
its armament of flowers.
And in quick time required
for a May Monday breeze
to sprint across Cambodia or a campus lawn,
four students are down.
M1 winds rifle through grief
among all things grounded and green.
Then, indeed, it is a silent spring.
No one left to protest
its fresh emergence
or Vietnam.

1971

One Indian, Crying

It is the single, glycerin-induced tear
that, arguably, launched—
a thousand recycling centers.

Wake of first Earth Day—
in a Keep America Beautiful television ad,
Old Iron Eyes Cody,
a Sicilian-American actor in Native American garb,
paddles his birch-bark canoe,
amidst ripples of discarded newspapers,
a tidal wave of maritime trash that gathers like dirty snow,
bunching, beneath runners of a sad, weary river-sleigh.

Behind his encroached rowing,
a skyline of burgeoning smokestacks, industry
hover in steel-clad horizon.
When beleaguered boat and passenger
finally reach the Styrofoam™ shore,
he is a helpless pilgrim to its foundered pollution—
wraps of wax and wasted food.

Alone, along a contaminated highway,
he is a forlorn feather, standing,
without acts of clean water, clean air—or even the EPA.

Insult pow-wows with injury.
A sack of drive-thru debris, tossed—
by a passing, thoughtless motorist—at his sopped moccasins,
the color of tainted turquoise, grease, and soiled deerskin.

No viewer is to know:
beverage corporations funded the commercial
to paint problem of climate tainting on the individual, not big business.
No eye is to descry of the hidden trade motives
buried within.

1972

An American in Munich

These were to be the "Cheerful Olympics,"
the "Serene Games,"
every logo, symbol, and security guard—
graced with a swath of peaceful light blue.

Each event, ceremony, and handshake—a flight of doves—
the antithesis of Hitler's stiff Berlin '36 propaganda—
not a single swastika
in any beer hall about the Bavarian town.

Covering the 20th Olympiad
from inside a television control room
brings its own look and lingo to the experience:
multi-camera commands, close-ups, roll cue, back on *The Bird.*

Things were going swimmingly
for media darlings Mark Spitz, Olga Korbut, Team Israel—
smiling and sporting
Borsalino brims throughout the spirited venues;

and things were sitting well
with rest of the viewing world, our audience,
who themselves, at home, were breaking records
with millions watching, safe in their living rooms.

The crew and I were about to close up ABC's studio shop
in the wee hours of Tuesday morning
when we heard pops, no, shots
coming from the sleepy Olympic Village.

With a round of bullets
sports became *news*.
Teams fought, not for gold,
but against the birth of terrorism.

An American in Munich

An able athlete could kick a soccer ball
from our position to the Israeli apartments at Connollystrasse
the housing complex where weightlifters, wrestlers, their coaches—
had been abducted, with two Israelis instantly killed.

There was no time to fly in a standard news team.
Arledge insisted this was our story to tell.
So, we wheeled a sluggish studio camera—outdoors—
set it on a hill, and pointed its lens toward an infamous balcony.

What we saw, what we showed—
all was shared with the stunned globe.
Germany was host. Israel was hostage.
The wounds of a post-war world ripped open, frame-by-frame.

I don't remember eating.
I don't remember anyone blinking.
A marathon of intensity,
the lunge-and-parry of dilemma against dilemma.

It was hours before we realized
Black September, the Palestinian terrorist group inside the complex,
could see what we were broadcasting—
every ground-floor negotiation, every stealthy police officer on the roof.

Then, terrorism became more than a new term.
It had a face.
A balaclava-clad man, with ominous slits for his eyes,
peered over the balcony, as if wanting to be seen.

I would lie
if I said his grim presence was not exhilarating.
He looked like a quiet watchtower
of pending power, impending doom.

An American in Munich

Daylight subsided. Darkness fell.
When I heard that helicopters were taking
the hostages and kidnappers to local airport, then a NATO airbase,
I felt it was an uplifting means to a tragic end. I hoped I was wrong.

Our camera crew stayed at the studio.
A grapevine grew throughout the control room and city,
threading misinformation to a willing ear.
The hostages are free. It's been confirmed by wire

Then, a faraway blast.
All faded to black.
Sports broadcaster Jim McKay relayed
to an impaled planet.

They're all gone.

1973

The Peace Sign vs. Smiley Face

These are rivals that circle one another—
the Peace Sign and Smiley Face.

And they compete for space
on denim, t-shirts, hot pants, biceps, plastic bags.

Both appear to be media darlings,
showing up at Vietnam War protests, burning-bra rallies—in a few folk songs.

Yes, they go their bout-rounds,
the disarming Peace Sign and mellow-yellow Smiley Face—

wreathing the "squaresville" world
in symbiotic tranquility and a nice day.

But, as both tokens are about to fade out—
like passing fads, hitchhiking jeans, smoke from a shared joint—

I'd say the Peace Sign will be the true, lasting ringer.
It's the one that can still give our globe—two thought-provoking fingers.

1974

I've Written a Letter to Nixon

August 1, 1974

Dear President Nixon,

Are you quitting? I overhead my parents in the kitchen. They were saying that you might be leaving your office. Will someone else take your stuff if you just up and leave? My dad told my mom that you're feeling the heat in Washington. I wish I could send you the spare fan we have in the garage. It still works. I turn it on when I'm sneaking popsicles out of the fridge and eating them out there. (Don't tell my parents.)

My folks talk about words I don't understand when they speak about you. Really tough words like *Watergate* and *impeachment*. Why does water need a gate? I know water can run, but would it ever run away? Where I come from, you keep cows behind a gate. They said Watergate was a hotel, too. Why were you in a hotel in Washington when you live in the White House? Did your wife get mad at you and throw you out for the night when you refused to sleep on the couch? My mom did that once to my dad. After that, our neighbor lady moved out of state and we never saw her again. And what do peaches have to do with the trouble you're in? Did you steal some at the Watergate Hotel and get caught? Don't you get your food for free since you're the boss of everybody? I've stolen an apple before, but I've never been imappled. And grapes too, at the grocery store. Oh, crap! I'm gonna get imgraped! Sorry.

Dad says there was a break-in with burglers. Don't you have a key to everything? Why'd you break into that hotel once your wife threw you out? Was the Hamburgler one of your burglers? If he was, why didn't you take hotel's hamburgers instead of those peaches?

I've Written a Letter to Nixon

The only person in my family who likes peaches is my best Uncle Max from Georgea. He is still missing in Vietnom. And I think you should spend more time finding him and stop stealing fruit. He used to buy me toy horses for Christmas. He never stole anything. He never broke into anything. The only thing he ever broke was our hearts because he's gone and we don't know when he's coming back. He promised to buy me a real horse when I got bigger. I believe him. I'm not so sure I believe in you anymore. Do you still have that cocker spaniel of yours, Checkers? Maybe you should give another speech about your dog, so people will like you again. If you quit this August, do we still have to go to school in September? I hope not.

Yours truly,
Little Pat Riot, almost 11 years old

(I put our address on the envelope. Don't rip it.)

1975

Shark!

My Bonnie lies over the ocean.

And I won't be swimming the shark-teeming Atlantic
to rescue or meet her reposed frame, there—any time soon.

I was eleven
when Steven Spielberg's *Jaws*
took a bite out of big screens across America.

And the fin-flick left emotional teeth marks all over me for decades to come.

I didn't go back to our local recreational pool until junior high tide.

It was if I could read beneath the water's surface—
and beneath that vicious liquid veneer circled a shiver of sharks.

And do you know whom I blame for all of this Great White gluttony?
That horny Chrissie Watkins in the nerve-drowning opening scene.
That saltwater sea nymph was one maritime sheet short of a full sail.
Chrissie, Chrissie, Chrissie—
She should've kept her clothes on and had herself another brewski by the fire.
That long-haired lily all but oiled herself in chum with those lascivious kicks.
And do you know what she gave that Great White besides both legs
and half her torso?
Confidence! That's right, confidence.

For the next two hours of treaded treachery,
we in the horrified, landlocked audience needed hot-buttered scorecards
to keep toast-tabs on the bitten be-gone:
yellow-raft shafted Alex Kintner, stick-fetching black labrador Pipit,
head-kebob local Amity fisherman Ben Gardner,
a boy scout leader in the estuary who, no doubt, earned his ADHD badge,
and Quint.

Shark!

Shark!

Quint, Quint, Quint—
I can still hear those barbed fingernails scratching
against the seasick-green chalkboard at town council.

Rub-a-dub-dub
Three reluctant men in *Orca's* tub:
the chief of police, an oceanographer, one sauced sailor—
all in pelagic pursuit of *Carcharodon carcharias.*

By the final act,
I was so shaking in my seat
that I didn't even notice that bomb-delivering, moonshine madman
was just that, both inebriated and insane.

What I did espy was a *fin-nomenon* in the movie theater.
A sellout cinema pool—all squirming, screaming, and shrieking
to each inner-tube thrashing,
tuba-induced stroke-note of John Williams' score.

Unlike the aforementioned devoured,
we'd all be back in the watch-water that summer—
with baited ticket, collective breath—
a bigger boat of popcorn,
grabbing all of courage and stupidity
we could muster.

Back to take in each frame like suspenseful sunshine—
until Brody and Hooper paddled to safe shore
while the seagull-seasoned waves roared—

Blockbuster, Blockbuster, Blockbuster.

1976

The Bicentennial...and a One, and a Two

I BICENTENNIAL BOUQUET

I say the word *flower*
& somebody, somewhere in America—delivers a smile.

We will need roses,
a soldier's bloodshed of red roses,
for the bicentennial bouquet.
The event is early summer.
Their thorned gorgeousness will be in plenitudinous bloom.

And white chrysanthemums,
mums the color of stark memory
to recall with vivid impressions
the valor of fallen service persons
lying beneath alabaster Arlington tombs.

At last, morning glories,
the hue of first light,
after an evening of forted battle
with formidable enemy
in a fireworks' display upon a spangled bay.

Then, I'm a-foot
like fleet-edged Mercury
to collect the official flower from every state,
sanctioned by each legislature—
one gavel, one petal at a time.

Fragrance of Florida, aroma of Arizona—a bicentennial is a bunch.
I need more blooms!
My sixth-grade math tells me to arrange 200,
I must accrue more than sweet 16 dozen.
Good thing flowers come in focal families.
(I'm off to pick a few distant & wild American cousins.)

The Bicentennial…and a One, and a Two

II THE POST-COLONIAL QUEST FOR AFTERNOON DELIGHT

I thought it was soda pop,
some new beverage with fizz and fun,
to refreshingly assist America
in celebration of approaching
bicentennial bliss,
a bubbly drink, perhaps cream-flavored,
white with foam.

Turns out,
Afternoon Delight was the lyrical Holy Grail of the 70s,
a subliminal metaphor for getting it on,
in the shades-drawn hours of early post-meridiem.

Everyone, from fife to drum, was in pursuit of its meaning.
It put a minted kick into the Spirit of '76.

And, according to the urgent words,
you had to *grab* it—like a sack of chips, or a set of keys,
almost as if you were on the run,
in quick-crack of not getting caught.

And the song had sky rockets. They were in flight. *Zzz-Mmmm….*
(The sound effects piddled off in a matter of seconds.
Isn't that always the way?) But there were sky rockets.

Yes, *Afternoon Delight* was the country's conundrum—
both popular and private, if not downright perplexing.

I was twelve at the time of all this patriotic pageantry,
on the cusp of puberty,
building my own concealed Uncle Sam
on the backside of state-saluting 7 Up™ cans.
What was all of this post-noon naughtiness to me?

I couldn't conjure up any Afternoon Delight even if I had
a state-of-art soda jerk and mixer.

1977

A Peanut Farmer from Plains

I like this new kid from Georgia, Carter.
He's a toothy goober on the soapbox; I'll give him that.

Peanut farming is much like the presidency.
You have to know the soil.
You have to care what goes in it, who treads upon it.
You have to seek out and nurture a warm climate
with long growing season.
You must deal with pests, fend off diseases.
You must have an eye for proper spacing, appropriate depth.
When no rain falls,
you must water the desiccated fields with your own sweat
and tears.
You have to possess instinct for harvest,
the proper time to dig and lift your seasoned seeds upon maturity,
release them from embryo-pods.
You must keep them all stored safe in the new, rarefied air.
You must provide just enough salt to provide a fair start.
You must coax them from darkness, with confidence,
to come out of their shells.

—in memory of Gerald Stern

1978

My Disco Diary

Dear Disco Diary,

I am in a funk.

My body feels like a broken vinyl record,
and my boogie caboose is depoted inside the county hospital.

The hazard happened last night
at a downtown Travolta-esque discotheque.

I was finishing my last disco finger to the final *yowsah* of a Chic tune
when some flare-jeaned clod hip-bumped me off my platform shoes.

I fell a full eighteen inches to awaiting hard floor.

Supine and writhing with abdominal pain,
I thought I was turning cyanotic, but it was just the ground tiles
changing from sparkle yellow to purple-diamond blue.

Suddenly, the infernal crowd pulled a retro *Love Train*
over my anguished, compromised anatomy...

...I thought I saw the world *flashing* before my eyes.
Turns out, it was the damn disco ball, with its myriad of mirrors
reflecting every blink of light in hip-hustling arena.

And now, Disco Diary, another bummer. Worse news.
The nursing assistant just left my room after telling me the diagnosis.

This is ABBA-awful.

I've ruptured my dancing spleen.

1979

Three Mile Island

Spring on the Susquehanna—
a malevolent mist lords the air.

Rumor and fear of exposure
meander through Middletown
like the muddy river itself.

My reactive family and I are all bunched
like panicked packages, hastened freight,
inside our '76 AMC Pacer, the color of alarm.

My son spits through his braces
that he's missing first track practice.

My daughter coddles a flute case
in her quivering lap.

My wife wonders if she should use
a manual can opener in our car.

This is the strife

It is somehow foolish, even cowardly,
running away from the invisible,
scurrying like thwarted flies
from the unseen.

Spring on the Susquehanna—
my daughter whistles a shrill lullaby
to her silver woodwind like it is her child,
my grandchild.

I imagine it with no eyebrows,
unable to grow delicate hair.

1980

Miracle on Ice

Colder than Olympic Center ice
beneath my puckish disc
is the glacial war
between these hemispheric bearers
of heated sticks.

I feel, not so much a fervid hate,
but a divided misunderstanding
whirl through Lake Placid's wintry arena,
beating on my black exterior
with each massive slapshot.

A freezing faceoff,
then body check after body check,
red lines, blue lines—
as expected, the strategic Soviets strike first—
but this is ice theater for ringed marvel.
This is slippery-slope stage for an ever-changing flame.

I glide, a playful flake, for my own glory.
I am impressed how the American goalie—saves me—
from wretched catch of pitted net.

If this is more than a mere hockey game,
then it is I who decides an outcome of international intrigue.

It is frozen-burger me who lifts and puts an exhilarated world
for three periods on my curved, slick shoulders.

Yes, I who net-settles, the Siberian dust
between hometown-hack amateurs and Russian professionals,
whether or not—a fresh laurel of the old, cold crown is to be worn.

I, who figures great in revelation of this monumental skate.
I, who puck-picks, if a miracle is born.

1981

Nancy Reagan at the Royal Wedding

This is about as alien-American as it gets.

Like a White House wallflower,
Nancy Reagan, the First Lady of the United States,
goes it alone
at St. Paul's Cathedral for the royal nuptials
of Princess-to-be Diana Spencer and Prince Charles.

Like a fairytale,
Mrs. Reagan quips to the press,
referring to herself being a guest
at the most anticipated social event of the twentieth century.

If, indeed, the world-spanning, broadcast vows are a fairytale,
then Little Orphan Nancy is a cross between Quasimodo and Snow White,
sitting by herself on wooden pew, six or seven rows back from VIP
action—sans Secret Service, no children, Patti or Ronnie, Jr., at her side,
her no-show husband, President Ronald Reagan,
at an economic summit in Ottawa, the obscure capital of Canada.

Did I say Snow White? Make that Snow Peach or Pink.
Fashion pundits around the globe debate the precise sorbet-sherbet color
of her three-piece James Galanos' design,
all pallor and pleats from scarf to shoes.

All she needs is a betting scorecard—
not to wager on the crown-jewel lovebirds—
but rather, because Fancy Nancy is dressed like she's one Slingsby Gin™ shy
of being the dowager ghost-countess of Royal Ascot or Grand National.

At last, the hat—
compared to all other *haute couture* in the sanctuary—
each sleeve and cinched belt in Anglican church fail,
for it appears First Lady Nancy Reagan is in tickety-boo company.
Upon her head balance the constituent states of Scotland and Wales.

1982

Let's Go Fly a Bike

Blue, not even Picasso blue,
ever had it so good, so poignant, so ethereal—period.

Silhouette blue
backdropped against a magnificent moon—

a zombie-caped boy, a frog-eyed alien,
a fly-away BMX™ bicycle built for two.

Grounded government cars pursue
their defiant pedals like back taxes.

Elliott Taylor and E. T., a tandem in trouble,
scale invisible cliffs, improbable mounts.

The crossbars of a bike are like
spars, make that, the spine of a kite.

Escape-room blue, befriended blue—
the extra-terrestrial, other world missed—euphonious bliss of *phone home.*

Nothing soars like cinema
when it elevates, captivates the seated, popcorn soul.

Up there!
It's a most-wanted bird! It's a crochet-blanketed plane!

It's an empathetic boy trying to unearth
a plant-pilfering enigma with all of a kid's might.

It isn't the length that Elliott will go to Reese's Pieces™
to make E. T. 's homesick blues turn askew.

It's the height.

1983

A Moonwalk with Michael

I had been stepped upon before.
Armstrong was first, in 1969, with a small footfall
to clear debatable dust
over who would be first person on Earth's moon.

And then there was Michael.
Ok. Ok.
The Pasadena Convention Center is no Sea of Tranquility.

But the Gloved One in dark sequins and leather loafers—

He had me at heel-toe

There is gravity on my surface,
yet I felt weightless, helpless on that palpitating stage.

My cycles were his cycles. His rhythm, my rhythm.
That glider from Gary, Indiana, took me through all eight phases.

He was the indelible gift; I was a roadie-lunar lift.

I didn't give a damn who Billie Jean was or wasn't.
Every comet-crashing crater in me was thankful
that unwedded mother triggered his world-class talent
to pulsate us all to another planet. Yes. Even Elvis was *hip*-story.

That dancing machine, MJ, put the *Moon* in *Motown.*

My man Michael Jackson had made the moment, the magic, the *Thriller*
record that was going to break record after record.

My only show-stopping concern as event applause, accolades
overcame hysterical arena in hordes:

What was my pale 2,000-mile-plus diameter frame going to wear
at next year's Grammy Awards™?

1984

On the Subway with Bernhard Goetz

If I look through the dark shaft
of his short revolver
as if a desire to perform fellatio
has overcome my fear, perhaps
his instrument will rise acutely
& miss killing thug-music
of this cruel, broken quartet.

The New York City Subway is, indeed a black bough,
a stream of amoral misfits,
unflinching fists, unfeeling waves—
electric hooligans panhandling for pennies
just to play an arcade.

The wired albino—
his passenger-temper
                    is trigger-nervous.
Sweat drips
            from his eyeglasses in December's brick cold.

The .38 starts spraying bullets
& spreading the news.

The four late editions, mere boys,
greased with a Smith & Wesson,
fold with the *Times*
to silver-stone floor with a clap.

Christmas just three stops away.
The Big Apple is goose-fat with vigilance
& vengeance.

...I'm leaving today.

1985

Live Aid, Deadly AIDS

What a difference an S makes.

The banners draped
beside both concert stages
at London's Wembley Stadium and Philly's JFK
speak out in shapes of Africa and valiant guitars
set to play, raise a little hell and a lot of money,
riff against famine
plaguing a faraway continent
with hollow scars.

The bulletin boards
congested with medical supply, renter-seeking cards
at London's St. George's and Philly's Penn Med
scarcely suggest one note, a letter
about an acronymic gay, unwanted affect—
much less post any effort to raise one pound or a cent.

1986

Christa McAuliffe at Liftoff

Were the great astronomers
ever compromised like this?

Ptolemy, Copernicus, Kepler, Galileo—

Did any of those learn'd sky gazers
ever have to lie supine on mission-control floor,
motionless, strapped
with lower limbs hoisted, fastened
as if at visit with long-witted gynecologist?

This is the real wonder, anti-glamour
of waiting-room hours before liftoff.

Something is too somber here, at peace,
too well-conceived, asleep, for the trip
to the blue multitudes—

My immobilized head feels like a fabricated pearl—clamped—
engulfed, inside a clamshell enclosure.

Only the male pilot and co-pilot, at this point, are allowed to move.

These royal orbit, lightweight suits feel fit for a picnic—
or pillow talk—
but will they withstand all pressure
once my colleagues and I are boosted
onward, skyward—toward the docket's rocket road?

And, this boom harness, it ejects, treks to a destination of—*where?*

Christa McAuliffe at Liftoff

Oh, Christa, stop it.
Think of your students—
the lunar lessons you'll teach them via closed-circuit,
the apple you promised to offer the spinster moon.

Follow your celebrity crew to the red-letter code.

And the nation at recess, on lunch hour, bursting with anticipation—

oh, I'm with them. I'm with them...

I'm about to explode.

1987

Girl Unwelled

If an 18-month
girl is to fall
into a 22-foot,
by 8-inch,
uncapped well,
perhaps it is best
to endure
such accident, duress
in Texas—
what with its
longhorn share
of drillers
and drills,
waterjet cutting
through bedrock
of limestone,
sandstone and chert,
a nation's tear,
a world of Pooh-prayers
engineered to
blast past
such rigid rift,
wrap a little lady
for home,
give the stuck honey
a lift.

1988

Flo Jo Nails It

Even the swiftest critters in South Korea
know by instinct, or near extinction,
that these Games belong
to the whiplash woman
with Hecate hair.

That is Flo Jo's gold; this is Flo Jo's Seoul.

That's what the Eurasian lynx thinks.
So swear the Korean magpie and Korean hare.

Neither the yellow-throated marten's
brisk black feet—
nor the peregrine falcon's
darting wings of speed
dare to enter the sprinter's
wind-rush arena.

Why even the Mongolian racerunner
with its whiptail form—
the agile Korean goral and briary wild boar—
each host-nation beast and bird
head for humble scrublands, mountain nest, or forest floor.

No native creature vies or contests
the slew of medal-moments in time
to stack and shine for Flo Jo,
the polished keratin quickie, celebrity of celerity.

All Ms. Griffith-Joyner needs is first-smoke sound of a starter gun—
to burst from blocks, run down a world-class field, finish off—everyone.

1989

Pieces of the Berlin Wall Across America

like fragments

of hands—scattered

strewn

from Wilshire Boulevard

to Madison Avenue

monolith fingers

Cold War lingerers

fractured tablets

grave commandments

a stretch of relic segments

graffiti hued

prop ghosts of impasse

at least, at last

you can walk beyond

West or East

you can get through

1990

Let Freedom Singe

How could you do it?

Burn her patriotic plumage.
Set her white stars ablaze on Capitol steps.
Cast her red stripes to cinders.
Simmer blue feathers.

When the symbolic smoke clears,
all that is left is a ring of regret.

Isn't it true?
All she ever did was wave at you.
Bid you, *Good morning.*
Watch over
your walk through a banner day
like you were her unfolding child.

Still, something's burning.
She must've struck a discordant chord in you.

And so, you strike a match.
Chant some incoherent cry of defiance.

But, it is she who will have the last laugh.

I guess they don't call it conflagration for nothing.
Her flames on Congressional grounds extend to national news.
They trigger spangled spirits; all Old Glory souls transfix.

Oh, say, you can combust the American flag, my friend.
But, come God-given sunrise, she will rise again.

She is liberty's bird.

She is freedom's phoenix.

1991

Oh, You Know, That Song

My favorite song of the year?
It's the one where the daughter sings with her famous daddy.
He's deceased.
Which makes it even more poignant and special.
Oh, what's her name? Natalie. Natalie Cole.
And her father, chestnut-roasting Nat King Cole.
Engineers extracted his voice from some 40 years ago.
Then, his silk crooning was layered with her angelic tones.
Music magic.
But, what was the name of that song?
Irving Berlin wrote it back in 40s or 50s.
David Foster produced the new rendition.
A virtual duet, they call it.
Incredible.
The title is on the tip of my tongue.
Miss Natalie swept the Grammys™ with it like dustpan to broom.
Memory escapes me like a prisoner swimming from Alcatraz.
Incredible.
Recollection slips like a banana peel on an oil slick.
Give me a minute.
It's a single-word title, I think, with four or five syllables.
Stress is on the third syllable, I'm certain.
The first letter is a vowel. The last letter is a silent e.
Oh, what is the name of that song?
My mind's an amnesiac swarm. (I blame Desert Storm.)
Regrettable.
I said give me a minute.
It will come. It will come.

1992

You Spell *Potato*, I Spell *Potatoe*

One must look out for silent *e,*
the soundless vowel,
its inaudible ability,
invasive way to bring down, well,
a spelldown.

Chalk it up to orthographic inexperience, linguistic idiocy.
Blame it on New Jersey.

Or perhaps Vice President Dan Quayle
should've steered cattle-clear—
of any elementary school or edifice,
any spelling be or bee
that might infringe or dismiss the Chief Deputy's dignity.

After all,
one fell Bush swoop—
of a leftover jellybean in the Oval Office,
and, by George,
this epitome of minuscule intellectual capacity
appoints judges, commands armed forces,
and pardons Thanksgiving turkeys.

Wo, make that woe,
is both the American education and political system
that has allowed such a mental aminoe, er—amino
to dominoe—no, domino— his way into the nation's prime think tank.

And to spud it all up with network cameras rolling,
the eyes of every couch potato—Davenport to Tater Town—watching.

What a fiascoe, er—fiasco—
from head to to...e.

1993

On the Pulse of Maya Angelou

Robert Frost recited here—
on the inauguration steps of the US Capitol, 1961.
America's poet faced east on the portico
to read for incoming President John F. Kennedy,
a new poem, "Dedication."
But the forenoon sun was too glaring, adverse
for the beloved bard to see,
so he opted to share an older verse,
"The Gift Outright,"
with lines and language of surrendering our souls
to the land beneath us.

Today, Maya Angelou speaks here
on the platform stage of the US Capitol, 1993.
Draped in blue Chanel™ coat (a gift outright from Oprah),
America's poet faces west on the front facing our National Mall,
to read for incoming President William J. Clinton,
a fresh poem, "On the Pulse of Morning."
Ms. Angelou, too, has faced glaring adversity.
But nothing in air, land, or sea is to prevent, alter, mute
her eloquent elocution of a rock, a river, a tree.
With a stern comfort, she personifies these natural geologies.
Nothing in her tone, tenor, or vehicle surrenders.
Stand. The rock commands.
Rest. Sings the river.
Root. Advises the tree.
Lift. Mold. Sculpt.

The day's break and brush offer an opportunity for endless artistry.
A brutish history may cling to the horizon's clad-in-peace sleeve.
But it will fall like the mastodon to the sunlit masterpiece forming.
This is America's beat, her rhythm and occasion
to put finger to wrist, thank God for one more day's sprig of mist,
then press two lips as if to say: *Good morning.*

1994

Bills, Bills, Bills, Bills

I've got no beef with the good folks of Buffalo,
never one to bad-name the Nickel City
a *Mistake on the Lake*;
but you don't need irrefutable evidence
or a plea bargain to admit:
This year has not been Buffalo's best graze in the grass.

Why, my missing pair of skid-mark underwear
has won as many Super Bowls.

Not even Jackie O (God rest her pearl-strung soul)
has incurred so many consecutive losses
as this empty bucket, basket, stocking, and trophy-case franchise.

And, if I am not mistaken,
was not Orenthal James Simpson,
that Heisman™-grinning running back,
a former Bills' superstar?

Poor O. J.
Just one consecutive letter more—and he would've been
O.K.

Now,
Buffalo's favorite son is on the sudden run,
and perhaps gaining ground for the Broncos.
(Oh, correction, he is inside a white Bronco. No comment.)

At any race or rate,
I see O. J. a free man headed back to New York state
once the California Highway Patrol juice down their chase
to end, at least for the crime being,
the media-frenzy fury;
and his legal Dream Team has sufficient time
to shrink some gloves to buffalo a befitting LA County jury.

1995

The Internet-ivity Scene

Come. We are not fools.
Let us be world-wide wise,
Netscape Navigators™.

There, above the Silicon Desert,
shines the Star of Amazon™
above an online, wireless sky.

Come. We shall doff these emblematic robes,
rid our heads of all mortarboards, academic tams,
ride on our low-friction mouses in surf-search of commercial scams.

We will find the bandwidth babe,
swaddled in fiber, lying in a router
with blue oxen, innumerable asses nodding logged-on heads.

Oh, magnificent Magi,
is this the window of wonder to a miracle?
No. But this is the Web.

1996

The Ransom Note for JonBenét Ramsey

I am the letter no parent wants to receive,
a series of handwritten demands
for safe release, return of a child—already paid for.

No, I do not know who did it.
My purpose is to command, speak—correction—
make that read, in clear imperatives—not to identify or bear witness.

You want to know *whodunit?*
Scrutinize the look and language of my three-page kitchen-stair dispatch.
Right away, you will notice a slip in diction.

Listen carefully. The note begins. *Listen carefully.*
Now, where is my red pen or liquid paper to better the letter?
Shouldn't that register *Read carefully?*

Listen carefully?
The last time I checked—I wasn't a phone.
I'm a few pieces of lined notepad sheets. And mother Patsy's at that!

Listen carefully!
This is a haphazard, unexpected utterance
as if someone were wishing they were a few boulders—elsewhere—
a full circuit of telephone wires away from suspicious house or city limits—
far enough away to cast a red-herring stone into the 15th Street oopsie.

I will print you this. *That. That. That.*
That black Sharpie™ that cursive-curved that obscure dollar amount—
I've been pressed by its thick black fingered-force before:
a list of weekly groceries,
the help's errands, you know, the usual household matter-of-facts.
Oh, yes, and a discrete memo-leaf ripped from my tab
a few holiday *ho-ho-ho* hours back:
an appointment for Little Miss Bump-n-Grind's
first bikini wax.

1997

Monica Lewinsky's Dress

It will be Clinton's midsummer confession—
not the stowaway, stained dress itself—
that will come clean,
absolved in cold, Congressional wash.

Ah, the dress,
electric indigo,
Han purple—
stored like a cherry preserve
inside a popped tart's Watergate closet—
so many spins and cycles
so many spews,
tricks of a telling tongue
to turn a nation aghast, blown-hard, & blue—

It hangs like a Lady Scandal-in-waiting.

If only her dry cleaner knew for sure—
If only the blue-moves garb were Bubba-seed free—

He is diplomatic daddy.
Theirs is the sealed dream.

Defeated donkeys are braying.
Elated elephants, thrumming.

When his executive stick withdraws,
he is Santa Claus—
and upon mishap lap of her gapped lapel
down the choked chimney,
he's coming.

1998

A One-Two Punch in Arts & Sports Entertainment

I OL' BLUE EYES

I cannot look a martini glass
in the blue-cheese, stuffed-olive eye
without hearing him,
the King of Croon, Sultan of Swoon—
though his preference of liquor,
a two-finger pour
of whiskey on a Ratpack of rocks.

Cast the Empire State Building
in velvet ropes of blue.

Halt the Las Vegas slots, casino wheels.
Dim the door lights of Caesars Palace.

Frank Sinatra has death under his skin.

And in the wee small hours of mourning,
a black bite into the Big Apple,
RIPs rip into romance

make it Hoboken certain.

When the end was near,
I hope Ol' Blue Eyes did it his way—
the privacy divider
of Cedars-Sinai Medical Center
the final curtain.

A One-Two Punch in Arts & Sports Entertainment

II AIR

Take a deep breath, roundball fans.
Air is about to retire—again.

His Airness's 48-inch vertical leap, 6 championship rings—all gone.

A dizzying reality,
the Bulls' main man, Minotaur
heads for other labyrinths, mythic pastures to conquer.

It's a tough chew, bitter butter syrup
at the pancake house on Randolph Street to swallow;
but I suppose the Windy City is accustomed
to phenomena blowing through it.

Oh, say it ain't so, WGN-TV!! Say it ain't so.!

Damn NBA™ lockdown! A player like Jordan has got to perform.
Like a no box-out on weak side,
the league is bound to rebound poorly from this.

Oh, Michael might be back for a third-time charm.
But this farewell from Chicago, the United Center—
it appears to be a slam dunk—
what with his #23 banner flying from proud court rafters,
and a bronze statue of the CEO of MVPs
firmly based in black granite on pedestrian atrium.

Hang time for desp   air.   Air is retiring again.

Over the city with Big Shoulders drapes a somber cloud.
Better call the Chicago Power Company.

The electricity is out.

1999

Fire and Ice—Plus One

A fire is fitting for spit finale—
or in second-thought line with Frost—
a global end-all, dripping to a hateful halt
in ice—
I don't know how to side with either's gorgeous fall;
I don't know the meaning of *suffice.*
My humble hope is if one destructive force
fails to decide which gorges over which:
The world does not end with a computer glitch.

2000

The Good, the Chad, & the Ugly

My love dumped me today
outside the polling booths at town hall.

Yes, I confess we were tick-talking over politics.

My gored heart is torn like a chad ballot,
clinging to a corner bit of my sternum—
like a storm door
                                        dangl-
                                              ing

but not completely punched out.

Now, I know what it is like to be in proverbial bushes.

The only sunshine side to all of this—this is Florida.

Perhaps the fall-out,
                    the whole demoting break-up exercise,
                                                  won't count.

2001

The Eleventh of September

September—

And the sky is wearing

White airplanes after Labor Day.

A good morning in America

Witnesses the fashion faux paus

Clashing into paired towers of world trade.

One, say two, false steps for humankind.

Pigeons stop their late-summer lovemaking.

A gray-winged squall plumes over Gapstow Bridge in Central Park.

A firefighter from the Bronx

Drops his egg/mayo sandwich, heads to lower Manhattan

To become a six-inch television screen hero.

And when his axe and mask arrive at hollow-hub

The Ground known

For "boroughing" such staggering stock numbers

Is Zero.

2002

Michelle Kwan Skates to *Fields of Gold*

How closely, it seems,
her surname is to *swan*—
down-feathered dip, —elegant, bent
crowning every cascade of air in arctic arena
like a frozen princess cygnet.

It is the post-Olympic exhibition
at low-lit Ice Center, a post-podium gala—
a flock of snow tears, a swallow of hours
after precious medals
hung from delicate necks,
then placed and nested for home.

Michelle Kwan appears
upon weightless, winged blades,
the favorite daughter of a fairytale, Ariel cloud.
She is wearing a sequined, signature Vera Wang dress
the color of once-upon-a-touch, Midas gold.
With flawless grace,
seamless, elysian precision
her limbs and lifts paint
a moving, lost Michelangelo masterpiece across the pond-hushed arena.

A gilded glider, an intimate twist—
she spins every jewel—any girl dreams of shapeshifting.

Slow tango, blue bolero in Salt Lake City.
Softness never had it so easy.

Shakespeare's aphorism disproved: *All that glitters is gold.*
Gold beyond ounce value, gold without brick limit.

At swan-skate's stroke-repose,
her pinioned palm-in-hand unfolds.
The entire world is in it.

2003

Weapons of Mass Destruction

Nothing. I've got nothing.

And I have searched, inspected every facility—
from Basra to Baghdad—
studied each broadleaf species
between the Tigris and Euphrates.

And nothing. Not a single stockpile.

True. I have unearthed some geological gems:
Neo-Assyrian gold earrings, a Roman-occupied coin, a clay foundation cone.
But nothing to implicate Iraqi intention
to subjugate our free world.

I followed, to commission red-letter, every adjectival suspicion.
Chemical. Biological. Nuclear. Radiological. Explosive.

Nothing. Mission and missile inscrutable.

Pickaxe depleted. U. N. intelligence-report cheated.
How can I go back—
without so much as a smudge on Iraq?

Oh, I abhor, disdain Saddam Hussein—
his insurgence on the Kurds, Kuwait.
He puts the teeth in terrorism.
Why, I bet he had a bite of, at least, a few floors of one tower at 9/11.
And I've no doubt his brutal, war-mongering ways are intended
to create a New Arabia beneath his umbrella's reign.
And still, I have nothing. Detect nothing.
Not even a footpath's pop-bottle bomb.

I don't know which is tuck-tailed worse.

Feeling flat empty, or being pat wrong.

2004

Lords of the Clean Sweep

Lord of the Rings: The Return of the King wins all 11 Oscars for which it is nominated. Boston Red Sex defeat St. Louis Cardinals in the World Series, 4 games to none.

Precious. Precious the pursuit of a gold ring—

whether it is cinematic quest for awards of One Ring

in caverns of New Zealand's Misty Mountains—

or the October hunt for a World Series champion's band

in dugouts of Fenway Park, fields of Busch Stadium.

And even more precious—

when the ultimate prize, possession is grasped, attained
without a fellow nominee's category scrape
or a rival league's best team hurling you one: nine-inning loss.

How scintillating, satisfying—
the fine dust of a clean sweep,
no mess, no misery,
not a poor soul's peep of defeat.

So, lords a truckload of trophies to *Return of the King.*
So, broken is Curse of the Bambino—Beantown's annual autumnal sting.

Clear the shelves at Wellington home of director Peter Jackson.
Give the Red Sox front office in Boston some pennant-room.

Precious—the arrays of consensus victory displays.
(Just keep both bastions away—from Grand Slam of Mount Doom.)

2005

Hurricane Katrina

I favor my name: *Katrina.*
It is Greek from *katharos,*
meaning *clean* and *pure.*

To me, nothing is more cathartic
than pure catastrophe.

I purge a dual disaster. Landfall arms akimbo.
Weapon of wind. Weapon of water.

When I drive my rains heavy to the levee,
the Lower Ninth Ward of New Orleans will be anything
but dry.

With my inland partners,
the Mississippi River, Lake Pontchartrain—
I head hard for Crescent City's high, holy ground.

Bigger than the Big Easy itself, I put the perish in parish.
Little Gem Saloon, irreplaceable family heirlooms—
I devastate, destroy monuments, memories most cherished.

To me, *Hurricane* is a title of earned respect
like *President* or *Madame.*

Ah, time to drench the French Quarter.
My storm surge seems to have a penchant
for vanishing ghost notes of jazz
in the key of why-oh-why.

The inimitable name is Hurricane Katrina.
Allow me to show your family—its new home—the Superdome.
And if you don't see what I mean—

here comes my eye.

2006

Is Wii™ for Us?

The kids and I just don't know—
Is Wii™ for us?

No doubt,
this is the year for gadget and gears.

And we certainly want to keep up this holiday season
with the Console Jones' on the block.

You see. It's my husband.
He's been hit with some joystick addiction, a gaming disorder.

If only the APA would diagnose it,
I would get him some treatment.

As for now,
I can't coax the bonked bastard
out of the damn basement.

First, it was Xbox 360™, some 365 days ago—
with its exclusive titles, online games.
Burt established, shall we say, layers of multi-player affairs.

Then, just a few weeks ago,
we took out a second mortgage for PlayStation 3™.
He's been downstairs, playing around, in Blu-ray™ heaven ever since.

Yes, my husband is in a threesome with Microsoft™ and Sony™—
and now—the Nintendo™ nymph.   (I can't beat those gaming gods.)

We want to fit in;
we're just not convinced—we want to Wii-Fit™ in.

By Christmas, I'm bound to end up
a Wiidow.

2007

The *i*Phone™ Calls on Em*i*ly D*i*ck*i*nson

Because *i* could not stop for Tech—
Tech k*i*ndly opted for me—
Four carr*i*ers held for my D*i*g*i*tal Self
i selected to r*i*de with AT&T™—

Sleek, dark smartphone—It knew no haste
And *i* had put away
My fl*i*p phone and my landl*i*ne too
For Its qu*i*ck Touchscreen.

We passed the School, where Add*i*cted K*i*ds strove (to text)
During l*i*t lecture— and— math
We passed long l*i*nes at Launch, the Apple Store
We passed the Cons*i*derable Sum—

Or rather—the Pr*i*ce—passed on to me—
Half a grand for 4GB brand—
Another Ben Frankl*i*n to double the data stack—
And both—with two-year contract—

We passed before a Palo Alto home that seemed—
A modest dwelling for the Ground—
Steve Jobs was scarcely v*i*s*i*ble—
Save H*i*s s*i*lver-and-gold gr*i*nn*i*ng from the Mouth—

i texted H*i*m what the *i* in *i*phone stood for—
He repl*i*ed a heap of *i*'s: *inspire, inform, individual,* and, of course, *internet*—
S*i*nce then, models—ser*i*es—Pluses—Pros—SEs—m*i*n*i*s—
Generat*i*ons have passed, and *i* could use some *i*ternal rest—

2008

America's First Barack President

He had us in Boston—
four summers ago, 2004,
delivering the keynote speech
for conventional party nominee
upon thundering Fleet Center Stage.

A junior senatorial candidate from Illinois, winsome
he sported a gleaming tie—
the color of water, the color of transparency,
the color of trust.

His words for children, the afflicted, the poor—
they were mesmerizing, uplifting,
up a patriotic flagpole.
body and spirit,
You felt as if he were hoisting you.

(I admit, for a chilling moment,
I forgot the name of the guy he was endorsing.)

He seemed more than a politician—like an invention, revelation—
a geyser from Midwest legislative chamber—up and coming.
As he spoke to the clamoring conventioneers,
it was if you could see a chair
from Resolute Desk in the Oval Office
being pulled out for him.

This election night, 2008 in Chicago,
Barack Obama stands as President-elect
to give his "anything-is-possible" acceptance speech
upon a Grant Park rostrum.

Red state, Blue state, I state, You state—
Obama is spearheading to Washington,
but he had the US in Boston.

2009

A Tale of Two Celebrities' Obituaries

It was the e-shock of grief; it was the e-shock of incredulity.

When the sudden news
of Michael Jackson's death
hit the Bose™ radio in my room,
the blues of *Billie Jean* beat it—
the *Gloved One,* come undone—
AP's mortifying report—
into doubtful walls
of my disbelieving, pop-pounding head,
causing a pin-up poster
of Farrah Fawcett to drip—
I mean, slip—
under my bed.

2010

Laughing Gull, Deepwater Horizon Oil Spill

This is the pits—of oceanic proportion.

Tarred, weathered,
my coat
of tuft-marble
turned to
prospector's guck.

Smudge of fuming horizon—

A tip of black
on brisk wings,
a sable hood—
suit me
to a tweeting tee—
but to be mired in goop,
a saturated splat—
in hideous, thick hue

is baseless.

Salting insult to injury
is a train of waves
slapping incessant batter
upon my muck-chained frame.

This is no way to treat
a bird of fresh sea.

This is no way to spill the company beans—

and, by gull,

this is no laughing matter.

2011

Joplin Tornado

If you look closely at a cloud,
that silver lining can be a twisting knife,
prepared to lodge \
                                        in a town's back.

A beautiful Sunday in May,
Graduation Day for seniors of Joplin High—
Pomp and Circumstance played,
tassels swayed from right to left,
diplomas held beneath grinning chins of pride—

then a procession of cars, the ride home—or to rented community halls—
garage doors touting posters of *Congratulations, Grad*—
parties of pulled pork, first beers, and talk of nothing
but bright future.

It is the hour of gifts and reception.

Then, an uninvited guest crashes through a blue gate—
EF5 just after 5,
its rain-wrapped encroachment destroys, devastates.

You'd trade your red Camaro stuck on Rangeline Road for a basement.
You don't know which is your worst nemesis:
the approaching funnel or waiting glass.

You duck. You pray.
You are sheltered by a story of two mice in a hurricane
that beehive-bearing teacher read aloud to you and your classmates
about the paradox of storms in third grade.

They pass. And they last.

2012

School Shooting 101

Someday, the death-toll body count will be 101,
your basic bloodbath;
and you'll need an unmarred classroom calculator
to do massacre's math.

Why?
Because it can't stop now—
That's why it's still happening,
will continue to happen.

Too many of the jig's pieces
either won't fit—or are too affixed.
It's about gun rights and gun wrongs—
our helpless accompaniment
to play along.

Be it Sandy Hook, or Columbine,
I can walk into any school
I want to—anytime.
I can bring any tool.
After all, I was back-staged bullied;
the front page will tell you: I was bruised.

I've got a round-of-fire excuses.
I don't' make mark.
I can't rate grade.
I mock at sports I've never played.

My dad owns weapons
he thinks he's got
locked away.

I'm harmed, so I'm armed.

School Shooting 101

Public education,
you've got too many doors,
not enough sensors or guards.
The breakfast line—school of fish in a barrel.
I've never hunted game in season,
but school in session isn't hard.

Haven't my collective casualties
surmounted the vanished of 9/11?
Haven't my hallway-horror strolls
brought you, again, to your "never again" knees?
I've got another cafeteria-hysteria
event to book—one near your district, neighborhood, and home—
one without airtight, airport homeland security.

You can keep terrorists off your body-scanned planes.
But what can you check, detect from backpacking me?

There is a lesson—or a handgun—in here somewhere.
Whatever the lecture—trust me—the teacher won't have last word.

Titanic may have crashed and sunk 100 years ago,
but this tragic habit is at only the tip of its iceberg.

2013

Symphony on Boylston Street

Terrorists snap.

Pressure cookers crackle.

Boston pops.

2014

Strike Debt

It is an act of altruism, not philanthropy—
a movement born from Occupy Wall Street.

Strike Debt.

When debt steps up to bonded plate
to take a swing at student loans,
hit on medical bills,
manifest a slugfest upon the interest infringed—

Strike Debt assumes the mound of High Ground.

It's a strategic game of direct action, change-up pitches—delays.

A godsend of goodwill,
Strike Debt is relief from a warm-hearted bullpen,
heating up to whiff debt—
at its greedy, grand-slam ripping seams.

Strike Debt leaves no runners stranded—
leaving a clear, clean playing field—
so folks can stretch to the next inning—
move along with their dreams.

2015

Acronym for Him and Him

Roy, do you see spectrum of rainbow colors on the White House?

Oh, yes, partner.

You bet, due-process, I do.

Groomed, we two to chapel's way.

Before today's supreme June milestone,

I never thought I'd certifiably say:

Victory won in court, to support America's gays, in all 50 states.

2016

Orange is the New President

I gaze in amazement
at the freshly-electorate-squeezed
President-elect Trump—
and wonder if I've taken enough vitamin C
for such a wee morning's dose
of reality.

Orange is the new president.

Orange, the color of glossy promises—
Orange, the color of belted rust—
Orange, the color of bleached goldfish—

Okay, I admit it. I confess. I'm a sore loser.
I was born on Hillary Rodham Clinton's Sweet Sixteen—
and hoping to use that certitude
for a chandelier's dance with her in the East Room.

I'll never get anywhere with Trump.
Even before he speaks—at this, his Hilton victory speech—
as he clears his throat—I'm intimidated.
I take one look at him, one listen—and want to fire myself.

I can't even afford the parking at Trump Towers.
I handle money like a greased heel handles a buttered banana peel.

God, it's late, I mean it's early—
I wonder what Hillary is doing for breakfast?

I hope he builds The Wall; the state of Texas could use the shade.

Orange is the new president.
It's no surprise he had groves of support in Florida; Florida grows him.
God—I hate to lose.
But, damn, that's an Orange Man. I bet he did well in Syracuse.

2017

#MeToo Movement

Rapport.

The predatory zoo, allegedly, opens with rapport,
banter and canter,
an understanding of score
between keeper and captive.

Then, a couple of "Archies" set in—above contract cages—
Hierarchy, Patriarchy—
to claim territorial advantage, elephantine eminence.

It's unhappy habitat, brushed business-as-usual
once trust is established
with a cubby secret—
or come-into-my-office, Cheshire-cat smile.

Led into the puma's paced lair,
it's a bit wooly and cryptic to an alpaca like you.
Then, hidden agenda's claw drops
                                        out of nowhere:

Breadcrumbs for bushmeat –
Do you want to keep your job, or not?

The causal beast is unleased: husky promotion for tusk-like erection.
That man is an animal!
But, then again, aren't you?

There is a press, then a paw-ful of petting on your silk panties.
Oh, if you were only back with your herd in the Andes!
You shriek for a carpool of witnesses—
                              but the watercooler has run 9-to-5 dry.
You purse your lips, think of your kids.
The groomed room speaks for you:
I'm ready for my close up, Mr. Weinstein.

2018

Tragedy at Table Rock Lake, Branson MO

I, for one, never trust anything *amphibious*—
amphibious food, amphibious features, amphibious cruises—pass.

But that is all rapid, rabid water under a Branson bridge,
the same witch water flowing over, into an air-intake hatch
causing the bad-weather bow's engine area to flood,
which led to subsequent, incremental sinking
of *Stretch Duck 7*, reduced to a mere paddleboat in distress,
perishing 17 of 31 tourist-travelers.

A watched pot may never boil. Evidently, a watched duck will sink.

By shoreline, by showboat, by sofa at home—
we, the transfixed, viewed from safe, calm distance
the gradual going-down
of a reinvented craft from World War II
into a whitecapped-seized, choppy swell
of inescapable hell.

Whitmanesque—in grand sweeps—the vessel vanished—
into the traitorous lake—foaming at the mouth, baring dogged teeth.

But, Captain, our forsaking Captain—the fearful trip was far from done.
It was Poseidon's curtain, Neptune's netted veil.
Stranded passengers sat on interior benches like sitting ____.
Fixated canopy sea-changed into encroaching tombstone.
The only thing unlatched, unleashed was unmitigated panic.
Life jackets floated as lonely drifts—
perhaps to save lives for another rainy day.

Is it true what the rocky gods say about drowning?
It strangles you everywhere, but the throat.
It is not enough to admit human error—
when such luckless blunder should've never been ticketed,
allowed to board the boat.

2019

Paradise Drossed

I

It is almost too easy—
the fiery irony of it all.

II

The city of Paradise
burnt to a California crisp.

III

The ghost of Fellini should film here.

IV

Cirque du Fumo, Circus of Smoke—
with Prometheus as protagonist-ringmaster
to summon all insurance agents
like trained seals on runaway red balls.

V

Circle the local water wagons. Send in the frowns.

VI

It took Titanic-like iceberg odds
for this devouring inferno to happen:

VII

In chthonic sequence, it all happened:

Paradise Drossed

faulty hook,
fallen power line,
a steel-tower induced spark,
low humidity providing light fuels a lift
drought's cornucopia of pageant-dry vegetation,
gale-force Santa Ana winds—to take the glow show from here.,
heat-lifting Sierra Nevada foothills,
citrus-sized embers hurling down tapering squeeze
of a convenient canyon.

VIII

Milton could pass through
to add a pyrotechnic passage, piece of baked clay or two
to his consequential, 17th-century volume.

IX

Dante himself might descend
into the charred core of destruction, environmental sin,
led by the moral strictures and guiding hand of Virgil

X

In wet treachery, it ends.
Final blazes of a hissing asp bite into flesh and pith of old town.

What Paradise has lost,
a pair of smokescreen speculators have found.

Virgil stands on ashes to receive his cue
from Fellini and his grand Italian crew,
then the Roman peasant-stock poet turns to Dante,
Milton, CNN, and network news—
as if to give a warm-climate welcome

to the Tenth Circle.

2020

Coronavirus on Maundy Thursday

a droopy ghazal

In nothing flat, longing's ache is a bend to rid red-bud queen to solstice arc of an iris.
A goddess, a rainbow, a flower—what more could spore from limbs of dignified
iris?

Leak of wind boasts, early spring, too soon for betrayal of disciples, invisible vines.
Shall I wait, in confinement of cold news, Upper Room, belated bloom of death-defied
iris?

At supper's sorrowing end is a door—what frame lingers at passage-pain's begin?
Perhaps grim pilgrimage relies in patient falls of stone set-aside, petrified
iris.

A broken petal of its lot spreads pus-easily like a residual dream—or convenient lie.
Thus, is the honor and horror of mortified
iris.

It appears, resurrects with dirge music, summon of blue, wintering strings.
Ethereal thief, concealed creep—so plays grave leitmotiv to mark wet feet of magnified
iris.

In 2020 hindsight, the ghost of Caesar bore a mask at ritual event, march of his ides.
Through a gauze gaze, his eyes stabbed, cried, and bled in vain for vilified
iris.

The drumming drops of water seen in Judas-sky are not those of my neighbor.
Still, we are full-circle kind, in harmony's fear, like a pose-frozen, terrified
iris.

A curse to breathe, cross to bear, from Matthew to John, rooted to rise, respire mid-air.
I weep in a garden, blinded spy—*Oh, Romans or Science, put a nail in it:* the crucified
V—iris.

2021

Cancel Culture Catches Up to the Statue of Liberty

At first,
I thought these histrionic heathens were scaffolding,
some patriotic pressures on my frame
in gracious name of preservation, renovation.

Then,
my stone pedestal began to quake.
Graffitied garments of my greened palla, stola
commenced to shiver-me-sleeves shake.

Indignant chains around my nimbus, diadem
tightened with Treason's intrepid stress.

Indeed,
I was losing liberty's just balance—
                        and my copper-plated dress.

I had arrived to America in hundreds of French pieces.
Apparently, I was one torque of tugged torch—(Angers Aweigh!)
to depart this home-harbor—in analogous, drenched fashion.

To Hell—
with your spangled flag, cracked bell.
What's left of you tired and poor, soulless clefts—
you artless, cart-before-horse assassins—
Give me a tempest-toss of a buoy—a strife line—
or, at least,
                                        one last splash of compassion.

2022

My Man Musk

I, too, enjoyed the limelight—
the pursuit of a Hollywood starlet,
braced handshake to secure multi-million NASA contract.

This new tycoon, Musk—
he has caught my death attention.

It is more than money—beyond limitless stretch of our investments.

The *e*-adjectives suit us best: *eccentric, eerie, elusive.*

If either of us has a heart,
at its bottom,
we are both inventors—
flying high on the wireless wire.

Why, Elon could be my living doppelganger to the breathing dollar—
sprinkling satellites, cryptocurrency among gaseous stars—
rethinking, re-zoning outer space,
pushing inert boundaries
with lucrative, electric alternatives.

A little tweet tells me,
the Dogefather has acquired a social-network platform,
renamed it *X,*
in an effort to create—oh, what is exact phrase in this solemn haze—
ah, yes, an "everything app."

The gossamer gossip among Houston tombs
suggests my man Elon is transforming the microblog arena
into a digital town square.

If so,
I plan to visit—at least in privileged spirit.
(They don't have any butterfly steak or fingernail clippers down here.)

2023

Ode to Swifties

Sirens of social media,
Namesakes to meteoric superstar,
You wouldn't dream of giving that Pennsylvania girl

Blank space

No matter how Piano Rapunzel
Treasures her high-tower privacy.

Screw the tattoo or bodysuit concert panties,
You crave Tay Tay's stowaway cardigan,
Or old scarf flung, sung in unison
To lyrics everybody knows *All Too Well.*

You send her chai spices, red lipstick, plush cats in lavender satin—
And torn-ticket kisses from an undisclosed row
Several sections, several more security guards away.

Eponymous obsessions,
You name yourself after her.
This takes *wannabe* one step further.
The fandoms of Madonna, Elvis, and MJ
Pale like anemic stiffs to Millennial Swiftdom.
And you know it.

A ticket to any stop on tour is hotter than a Del Norte County wildfire.
Still, you follow her, not for hours, but eras—
Each glitter-sequin, twirl of boho dress.

Generational groupies,
Climbing for your due place up the Taylor-totem pole
With fan accounts, hashtags, arts and edits of her likeness,
Incessant arguments over Blondielock's best album of all time—
Online, Swifties fanatically searching court records
To change each of your birth years to 1989.

2024

The Caitlin Clark Effect (in Nine Three's)

Humans have a desirous tendency
to attend things closely guarded:
the Hope Diamond, Louvre Museum, and Caitlin Clark.

Few people know this,
but the "Little Engine That Could"
from original storybook is a she.

When boy engines poofed or pootered out,
it was her blue plate
that pulled freight and weight.

That's the best that I can do
to explain this social psychological wo-manifestation—
the Caitlin Clark Effect—

her black-and-gold # 22 jersey
that created such a wide fanbase,
cut an even wider commercial cloth.

Who knew such a deadly three—from beyond corporate logo
would swish-and-serve
as flame to our merchandise-eating moth?

Gone is the patriarchal mastodon
whose stone existence caused vacant arenas,
whose chauvinistic husks honed cheap seats.

That girl from Iowa is queen-doyenne of ESPN.
Connecticut critics, who Connecticut-continue to doubt her:
Imagine the WNBA or 2028 Olympics without her.

The Caitlin Clark Effect, in essence,
turns Iowa's, make that America's, GDP from corn to bread$.
(But then again, I thought Nelson Mandela was already dead.)

2025

We the Papal

White smoke blows from a work whistle atop a Chicago meat-packing plant…

In Italian,
apple pie is *torta di mele.*

All other American staples:
baseball, hot dogs, even *Chevrolet*—translate, literally, the same.
(Easy. The pontifical adjustment should a piece of Atomic Cake,
a walk in Lincoln Park.)

Yay! Wow! Hooray! Yippee! Woohoo! and Whoopee!
By hook and line of St. Peter, the new pope is American!
Not Argentinian, not blue-blooded European, but red-blooded American—
as American as Black Friday shopping, dryer sheets, toaster pastry,
Cinco de Mayo—our boy Leo is as American as Americans say *cheese!*

The conclave of cardinals has smoken—er, spoken.
It's the kid with the Comiskey Park grin.
Upon his vestments of red pellegrina, gold-embroidered stole,
I do declare I see a pair of White Sox!

Like Bad, Bad LeRoy Brown
this Holy Cow Father was born and raised on the south side of Chicago.
(If only Dillinger, Robin Williams, Jim Croce, John Belushi could Holy See this.)

Pope Leo XIV—
Pope of Big Shoulders, Pope via Villanova, Pope with an L-train pass.
Why, the entire USA is assuming Holy See residency.
It sure frames a pretty picture above a Flexsteel™ sofa: *Rome Sweet Rome.*

Hold the ketchup! Hold your horses!
Reserve a Sistine Chapel, blessed-and-bound, double-decker bus.
The Vatican City is about to become Vacation City.
And you can bet your St. Basilica communion wafers and wine,
we're bringing tackle football and six packs of brewskis with us.

Epilogue: Otters of the American Revolution

Otters of the American Revolution
gather at the Ottomac riverbank
just outside Ottington D.C. (Dry Creek)
to honor their ancest-otters

who swerved otterably

during the American Revolution
some 200-frisky years ago.

Old Glory blessed, holding collective breath
from Ottawa to Ottumwa—(Go Bulldogs)
these otters bother
to hunt and groom the Worldwide Webbed
to applaud with forepaws
their Founding Otters.

This year's Hall-of-Fame Otteree: Hairy Otter
(of Squint-eyed Friction novels)

My how the years have whiskered away in a furry—
make no blubber about it.

Like Greek Odysseus himself,
these courageous critters have sailed—
their own Otter-sy.

Be it by romp or by raft—arranged,
unaffected by climate change—
they get by with a little kelp from their friends.

Mudslide and true, for the Red, White, & Blue,
Patriots of the Back Paddle
from swim to shore—
to go where no pun
has ever punned before.

Made in the USA
Monee, IL
16 October 2025

32180874R00164